8/22

P9-CBB-663

Alias
Anna

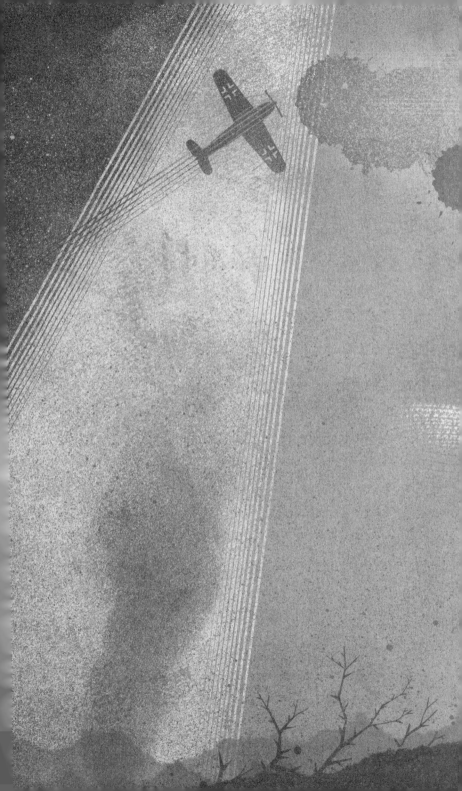

ZHANNA ARSHANSKAYA: A BIOGRAPHY IN VERSE

Alias Anna

A TRUE STORY OF OUTWITTING THE NAZIS

SUSAN HOOD
with **GREG DAWSON**

HARPER
An Imprint of HarperCollinsPublishers

Alias Anna: A True Story of Outwitting the Nazis
Text copyright © 2022 by Susan Hood and Gregory Dawson
Interior and map art © 2022 by the Balbusso Twins
All rights reserved. Printed in the United States of America.
No part of this book may be used or reproduced in any manner
whatsoever without written permission except in the case of brief
quotations embodied in critical articles and reviews. For information
address HarperCollins Children's Books, a division of HarperCollins
Publishers, 195 Broadway, New York, NY 10007.
www.harpercollinschildrens.com

Library of Congress Cataloging-in-Publication Data

Names: Hood, Susan, author. | Dawson, Greg, author.
Title: Alias Anna : Zhanna Arshanskaya: a biography in verse : a true
story of outwitting the Nazis / by Susan Hood with Greg Dawson.
Description: First edition. | New York : Harper, an imprint of
HarperCollinsPublishers [2022] | Audience: Ages 10 up | Audience:
Grades 4-6 | Summary: "An inspirational nonfiction novel-in-verse
about Zhanna Arshanskaya, a young Ukrainian Jewish girl using the alias
Anna, whose phenomenal piano-playing skills saved her life and the life
of her sister, Frina, during the Holocaust-from award-winning author
Susan Hood, with Zhanna's son, Greg Dawson"— Provided by publisher.
Identifiers: LCCN 2021025190 | ISBN 978-0-06-308389-9 (hardcover)
Subjects: LCSH: Dawson, Zhanna . | Women pianists—Biography—
Juvenile poetry. | Child musicians—Biography—Juvenile poetry.
| Jewish children in the Holocaust—Ukraine—Juvenile poetry. |
Children's poetry, American.
Classification: LCC ML417.D23 H66 2022 | DDC 786.2092
[B]—dc23/eng/20211012
LC record available at https://lccn.loc.gov/2021025190

Typography by Laura Mock
22 23 24 25 26   PC/LSCH   10 9 8 7 6 5 4 3 2 1

First Edition

R0463293153

*For grandchildren who dare enough to ask
and grandparents who care enough to answer—S.H.*

*For the Jewish children of Ukraine
who did not live to read this book—G.D.*

A NOTE ON THE NAMES:

Russian names have different endings for males and females. The family name is the father's name: Arshansky. But Zhanna and Frina would be known as Arshanskaya.

The names of Ukrainian places in the book are the historically accurate Russian spellings in use at the time. Since then all places in Ukraine have carried Ukrainian spellings on official state documents such as maps showing Kharkiv, Kyiv, Drobytsky Yar, Lyubotyn, Kremenchuk, and so on.

Music gave us so much,
to escape even for a few moments to a "normal" world.
Music allowed us a complete disconnect
and emotional escape from the daily life.

—GRETA HOFMEISTER,
a child in *Brundibár* children's opera at the
Theresienstadt concentration camp (Terezín)

Can music attack evil?
Can it make man stop and think?
Can it cry out and . . .
draw man's attention to . . .
vile acts to which he has grown accustomed?

—DMITRI SHOSTAKOVICH,
Soviet composer

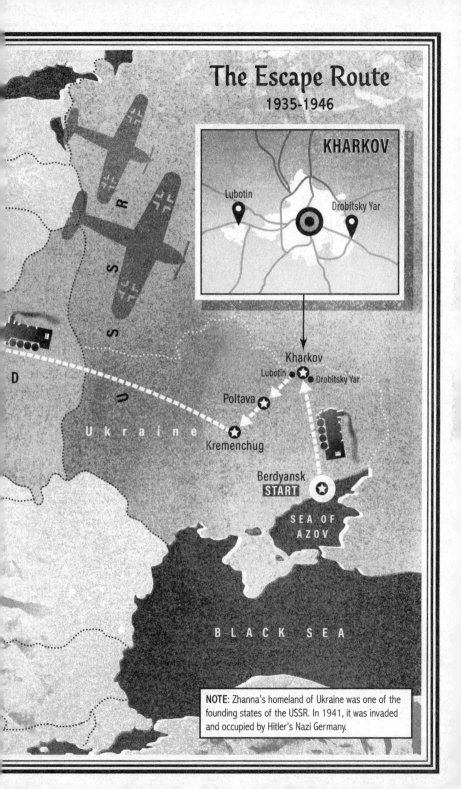

NOTE: Zhanna's homeland of Ukraine was one of the founding states of the USSR. In 1941, it was invaded and occupied by Hitler's Nazi Germany.

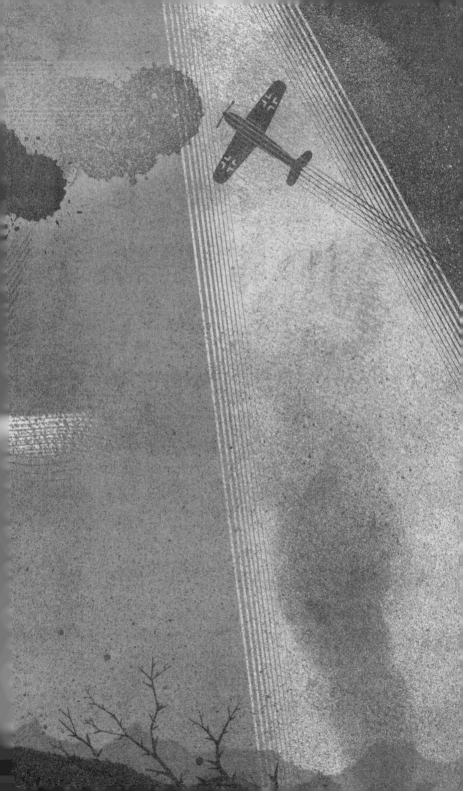

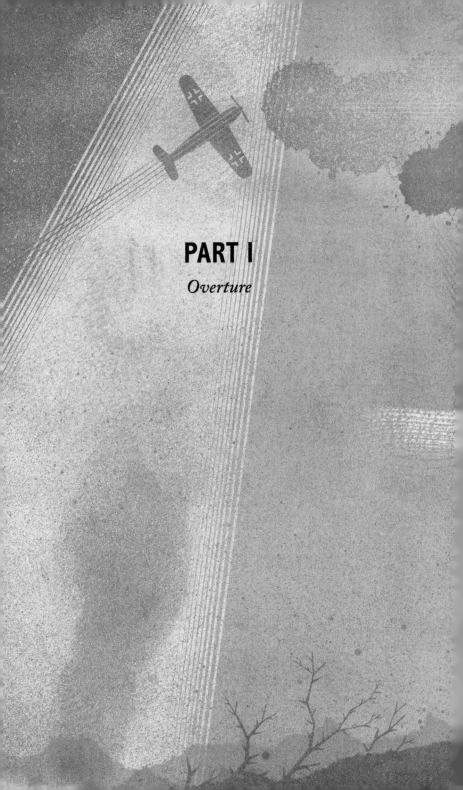

PART I

Overture

A LETTER

Dear Grandma (Z),

Hi, how are you doing? I hope everything is going well for you right now. I am writing this letter for a school history project we are doing.

The project is to find out as much as possible about our grandparents and what was going on when they were 13 years old. . . . Some specific things I would like to know are what life was like overall in 1940? What was your home life like?

Also, what are some major world events you remember around that time? I would really appreciate it if you could write me back and tell me some more about your life. I look forward to hearing from you, and hope to see you soon.

(Happy Holidays) ♥

Love,
Aimée Dawson

WHEN ZHANNA WAS AIMÉE'S AGE?

How could she answer her granddaughter?
Long-buried horrors,
stifled sorrows
Zhanna had pushed away,
pushed down,
        now came rushing up like bile. . . .

    rifles

soldiers   the pit in her stomach

        shoving

    bitter cold   icy stares

      families lined up

    little children   grandparents

people laughing, pointing, taking pictures

        humiliation   confusion

What had they done?   Where were they going?

a bribe

a whisper

running

running

running

ESCAPE!

She had to hide,

but where?

but how?

A NEW NAME

She'd hide behind
a new identity—that was it.
She wouldn't be Zhanna.
She'd use an alias.
She'd drop the *Zh* from her name
become Anna—
smaller, plainer,
more able to blend in.
She'd begin again.
     A for Anna.
        A for alive.

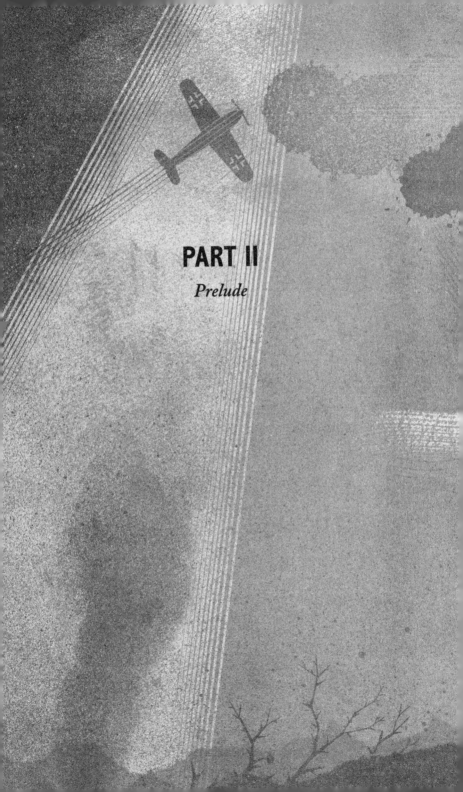

PART II

Prelude

WHAT'S IN A NAME?

Zhanna's real name
came from literature.
Her mother, Sara, an avid reader,
filled her home's nooks with books,
authors known the world over—
Tolstoy, Shakespeare, Twain.
She chose her newborn's name
from the Russian translation
of Mark Twain's *Joan of Arc*—
that fearless young woman warrior
clad in white armor,
the beloved heroine of France.
Sara chose the Russian name closest to Joan.
     Zhanna.

     Zhanna Dmitrinov Arshanskaya
     Born April 1, 1927
     Ukraine, USSR
         Born fearless.

A CANDY-COATED CHILDHOOD

Zhanna woke every day to sugary smells—
her papa concocting his own special spells
of fruit-flavored candies and fine caramels.

He'd fire the stove, set kettles to boil,
mix butter and cream with sugar and oil,
and keep careful watch so nothing would spoil.

He'd market his candies outside on the street.
He earned just enough for his family to eat.
But for a young child, life with Papa was sweet!

THE HUM AND HUB OF THE HOME

Sweet smells, sweet tastes, sweet sounds!
When Zhanna's papa wasn't concocting candies,
he was conducting concerts.
A self-taught violinist,
Zhanna's papa played
at family weddings and
downtown for the silent movies from America.
With the extra income,
he invested in the best—
a small upright Bechstein piano
shipped from Germany.
It became the beating heart of their home,
their sacred shrine,
and the source of much joy.

Music was the higher power in the Arshansky home.

The state condemned belief
in their Jewish religion,
in *any* religion—
in any greater power
competing with Communism
so music was the spiritual refuge

for the Arshansky family.
The violin and piano were
where Zhanna grew up to find
tradition, prayer, ritual, and devotion.

BURDENS AND BLESSINGS

No, the Arshanskys
didn't have a lot.
They knew what it was
to have and to have not.

NO
hot water
indoor plumbing
refrigeration.

BUT YES
a small rented house
two grandparents
two parents
one little girl
and in two years' time,
another blessing,
a second daughter—Frina.

NO
steady electricity,
BUT YES
their home was charged,
lit and lively

with a love of
music,
literature,
and each other.

Zhanna grew
just as her mother
had predicted she would
when she named her.
Like Joan of Arc,
Zhanna was
blessed
burdened
dauntless.

FEARLESS

Most mornings,
long before her parents awoke,
three-year-old Zhanna
was up and out the door,
wearing whatever she could find.
She couldn't reach the latch
on the front gate
so she would find a way
to climb up and unlatch it.

> *I had to go where I had to go.*
> *I had to see what I had to see.*
> *I was born busy—eaten up by curiosity.*

There were no cars,
only horse-drawn carriages and a few bikes
in her small resort town of Berdyansk
nestled near the warm waters
of the Sea of Azov.
Zhanna wandered the cobblestoned lanes
lined with flower-filled acacia trees.
She peeked in shop windows,
and dabbled her bare toes
in the water at the beach,

where she might spot a dolphin.

> *Nobody ever bothered me. . . .*
> *I didn't stay anywhere very long.*
> *I was investigating.*

For company, she might meet
sandpipers, swans, herons,
ducks, geese, seagulls, and lapwings
who warbled, trilled, and called
their morning melodies
against the rolling, rhythmic beat of the waves.

Zhanna didn't swim.
She knew that she wasn't allowed to.

Instead she would sit on the ground
and collect seeds, shells, and little pebbles
to take home to sort and classify.

There was only one thing that frightened Zhanna.
Caterpillars!
She hated the way they wiggled
like tiny snakes.
She'd hurry away
screaming like baby Frina,

her adorable, golden-haired,
one-year-old sister
who took so much
of their parents' time.

Zhanna's favorite shop
was the apothecary,
where she watched transfixed
as the pharmacists,
white-coated wizards,
measured and mixed
their magic elixirs
in white porcelain jars.

She looked at the potent decanters
with such envy and wished
she had a few of her own.
What potions she would brew!

The summer air
mixed the sweet scents
of roses and lily of the valley
with the salt of the sea
and the brine of the fish—
sturgeon, turbot, gobies, and perch—
laid out at market.

Zhanna breathed it all in.
It filled her up.

> *I had the best place to live, the best city,*
> *ocean. All of this was mine.*

At the end of the day,
Zhanna might be carried home
by a policeman to her worried parents
who had not been able to find her.
Try as they might,
they couldn't stop
their young explorer.

> *Nothing could stop me.*

MUSIC WAS THE MAGNET

One day while wandering,
little Zhanna stopped
at the sound of
a small band approaching.
The music was low,
mournful,
heartbreaking.
Down the street
came a horse-drawn wagon,
bearing what?
As it passed, Zhanna saw.
A coffin.
Zhanna gazed up, wide-eyed,
at the bearded Orthodox priests
leading the way,
each in a splendid robe
and capped with a kamilavka.

She stared at the forlorn faces of the family
who kept a steady, solemn pace
as they marched behind,
in time with the music.
She simply had to follow.
Down the street,

up the steps,
into the church.
Since Zhanna's family wasn't religious,
she had never met a rabbi
and never entered a synagogue.

So this Russian Orthodox Church
was the first time she had slipped inside
a house of worship of any kind.
It was

> *gilded, lavish.*
> *There were icons everywhere*
> *and mosaic windows. . . .*
> *I felt like I was already in heaven.*

From then on,
Zhanna would follow funeral marches—
any funeral—
when she encountered it
on the streets.

> *The music was the magnet.*
> *It broke my heart every time.*
> *I would get the biggest tears*
> *and would walk with the family,*

crying for their relatives.
I was absolutely obliged to go.

Just as her papa worshipped his symphonies at home,
music was the Divinity Zhanna was drawn to.

LULLABY AND GOOD NIGHT

Evenings, after a good Russian meal
of borscht, herring, or meat pastries,
Zhanna waited
in the violet twilight
on the street corner
for her papa's good friend Nicoli.
She'd run to him
and he would toss her, giggling,
      up and up and up,
high in the air
and carry her inside.
There he and her papa,
two self-taught musicians,
settled in the living room,
brightening the night
with piano and violin
played beneath
pungent kerosene lamps
or by flickering candlelight.
Zhanna sat on Nicoli's lap,
her pudgy dimpled hands
hovering over his
as he played piano,
while the genius of Rossini,

Bizet, and Tchaikovsky
struck chords deep within her—
melodies, harmonies, tempos, and tones
that would last a lifetime.
When it was bedtime,
Zhanna refused to leave the cozy scene.
Her parents dragged some bedding
into the living room
and then Zhanna slept,
her dreams underscored
            with the operas of old.

A HERO AND A PAL

Zhanna adored her parents
in different ways.

> *There was no bigger hero in my life than*
> *my mother. She was a quiet, delicate*
> *person, beautifully mannered without*
> *malice ever to anybody. She was a superb*
> *housewife, wonderful cook, and mother.*

Zhanna and her papa were pals.
They looked alike, acted alike—
both outgoing, adventurous.

> *I was like a daughter, brother, sister,*
> *everything to my father. He hated to leave*
> *home without me.*

Dmitri hoisted Zhanna up on his shoulders
and took pride in introducing
his pretty, chatty, insatiably curious
daughter to the world.
They'd treat themselves to
waffles and ice cream on the street.
Each outing was an Event.

Zhanna learned that the people she met
on these father/daughter outings were good to her,
that people were charmed by her.
She adored her papa, but she was smart enough
to get away with doing whatever she liked.

> *I played rings around my father. I arranged*
> *everything so that I wouldn't be punished.*

These outings became fond childhood memories.
All except one.

NO LAUGHING MATTER

Zhanna's parents took her
to see a silent movie one night
at an outdoor theater near home.
As usual, Zhanna rode
on her papa's shoulders all the way.
Baby Frina was left with her grandparents
and Zhanna had her mama and papa
all to herself.
It should have been a family fun night.
The silent movie was American,
a slapstick comedy,
starring two men looking for laughs.

> *One was very little and the other was*
> *endlessly tall. When they started hitting*
> *each other, I started to scream. I got*
> *hysterical and was crying so hard. There*
> *were no guns and no sound, but there was*
> *a fight and I couldn't take it.*

For Zhanna, violence—
even pretend violence done in jest—
was no joke.

KINDERGARTEN?

If Zhanna's parents
thought kindergarten
would stop her wanderings,
they were mistaken.

> *The children were supposed to be something*
> *like my age, but I was like a giant there.*
> *They had dripping noses. It was disgusting!*
> *I thought it was the most boring thing in*
> *the world. The teachers paid no attention*
> *to me because I didn't need their help. I*
> *already could count, and read, and add, and*
> *subtract. I simply hated it.*

Zhanna's preferred teachers were back home.
She'd cuddle up with her papa
as he taught her the musical scale
and told stories of the great composers.
She'd listen to her mama read
Russian basni—fables—or poetry.
As a family,
they'd gaze at the geography maps
her parents spread out,
laying the whole glorious world

of rivers and mountains and oceans
at their young explorer's feet.

Zhanna beamed in the warmth
of their attention.
She took in her parents' words and ideas,
just as a prism captures sunlight
and reflects all the colors of the rainbow.

In the mornings, Zhanna's walk
to school grew longer and longer
until she simply stopped going.
        The real world was much more absorbing.

TESTING

Zhanna tried her pesky best
to put her family to the test.

Was Grandma knitting? Off to rest?
Time to stir the hornet's nest!

> *My grandmother was a person of limitless*
> *patience. One day she and I were the only*
> *ones at home. Grandmother was knitting*
> *and . . . I decided to test her patience*
> *and tolerance. I picked up a heavy brass*
> *mortar and pestle and started beating them*
> *together to see how long she could stand it.*

No matter how she teased and pressed
her grandma calmly stood the test.

Never once was she distressed.
Never once did she protest.

> *It was I who had to give up when I lost my*
> *power. She kept knitting as though there*
> *was peace and quiet, almost as though she*
> *knew exactly what I was trying to do—*
> *exasperate her.*

A match of wills! Gram aced the test.
That little pest was most impressed!

BEAUTY AND THE BEAST

To Zhanna, her baby sister
was just that—a big baby!
Frina couldn't play her games,
she couldn't be bossed around,
she couldn't even talk.
For Zhanna, a precocious preschool adventurer,
Frina was simply no fun.

*Frina was the most gorgeous child you
could imagine, with long, golden curls. But
to me, she was always a baby. I wanted
her to speak to me sooner than she could.
Once we were sitting in the sandbox—I
was four and she was two. I got very mad
because she did not follow what I wanted
her to do. I threw sand in her face and it
got in her eyes.*

*I can't stand the thought of what I did. The
guilt can last a lifetime.*

PIANO LESSONS?

Little Zhanna clearly had a mind of her own
with the spirit—and arrogance—
of a galloping thoroughbred.
She needed someone to rein her in,
to corral her energies.
Zhanna's papa thought
music might give her some discipline.
He had just the teacher in mind—
a family friend and pianist named Svetlana.
He invited her to dinner.

He explained their predicament:
they needed to get Zhanna off the streets.
He begged Svetlana to take her as a pupil.
Svetlana looked at Zhanna's small chubby hands,
a far cry from the fine fingers of a pianist.

Zhanna ignored their conversation.
She was busy.
Her chubby fingers were just the thing
for dipping in butter on the table.
She swirled them around
in the golden goodness
and licked them one by one.

Svetlana looked
from the cheeky, self-absorbed child
to her doting dad,
clearly at his wit's end.
She reluctantly agreed
to take the child as a student.

It wasn't long before Zhanna bucked.

> *The lesson was every day and I was*
> *to walk there. It was just to send me*
> *somewhere because I quit kindergarten. I*
> *would take two hours to get there—about*
> *three blocks. . . . I didn't want to take piano*
> *lessons. I knew the notes. My father taught*
> *me. . . . I knew the staff line. That's it,*
> *I decided. I'm not going to [learn more]*
> *because it's no fun.*

Whenever her teacher gave her homework,
Zhanna took the assignment home
and stuffed it in the stove.

JOY! TOYS!

Zhanna may have scorned
practicing scales or learning ledger lines
BUT
she was charmed by her piano teacher's
adorable two-year-old son
AND his many toys,
so unlike Frina's dolls.
Often by the time Zhanna arrived,
the teacher would have left her son
with his nanny and gone off
to do her errands.
She was not about to sit around
waiting for her testy student.
The battle of wills had begun!

The children would play together for hours.

Zhanna only sat down to play piano
when Svetlana arrived back home.
She watched Svetlana play
and slowly,
          steadily,
                came to love and admire her teacher.

My teacher was like a goddess to me.
I thought she was a perfection of a human
being.

Svetlana disciplined Zhanna,
rapping her arm with a pencil
when she wasn't paying attention.
But Zhanna didn't mind.

> *She couldn't do wrong. I was in awe of her.*

The music swirled
through the warm afternoons,
both soothing and stirring
the impatient child.
She listened.
  Intently.

> *I was interested in music. I didn't want*
> *all those lines and things, no! I'm really a*
> *listener. That's where you learn the music.*

Chopin, Brahms, and Beethoven
soon conjured up
all that was good in the five-year-old's life—

birdsong mornings
at the beach,
animated afternoons
with Svetlana, her boy, his toys,
enraptured evenings
with her papa and his friend Nicoli.
It was her heart
that made Zhanna's fingers move . . .
and improve.

ALL EARS

Zhanna's father was eager
to showcase his rising star
and her many gifts.
He invited family and friends
to small concerts at home
where guests marveled at the sizable talent
in someone so small.
If they were impressed,
well, that was nothing.
Dmitri, master of ceremonies,
had another trick up his sleeve.
With a bang of the shutters,
he would block out the sunlight,
and have Zhanna play in the dark.
Whether Dmitri knew it or not,
this was how Chopin
taught his own students.
Learning to play in the dark,
pianists can show off
their memory of the music
and their mastery of the keys.

After Zhanna played,
applause filled the room,

marred only by hiccuping tears
coming from the laundry room,
where little Frina, limp as a wet dishrag,
hid in a basket of dirty laundry.
She wanted to be like her older sister—
aglow with the grown-ups' praise and attention.
It would take another year or so,
but she would get her wish,
for Frina, too, had a gift for music.

An astounding gift.

OPPOSITES

While Zhanna was flitting about,
winging her way into the world,
basking in the glow of her papa's devotion,
Frina stayed home cocooning—
wrapped up in her mother's love,
swaddling her dolls.

> *I never played with dolls. I didn't know*
> *what to do with a doll. When I got home,*
> *I would get all kinds of little bottles and*
> *pretend to do chemistry.*

The sisters were so different
they didn't spend much time together
as little children.

> *[Frina] led a very isolated life as a child.*
> *I was home very little. I was too busy. I*
> *always thought [Frina seemed] not two*
> *years, but ten years younger than me.*

ONE YEAR LATER

When Zhanna was six,
her teacher Svetlana appeared
at the house with news:
she would like permission
for Zhanna to perform
Bach's Two-Part Invention No. 1
in C Major on the radio.

Dmitri was gleeful.
His dreams for Zhanna
were coming true!
Zhanna dressed for the occasion
and walked hand in hand
with her proud papa
to the radio station studio.
There she encountered
a grand piano for the first time.
It was massive—so much more imposing
than the compact upright at home.
The grand piano's raised lid,
like a raised eyebrow,
might have seemed to question Zhanna's ability,
but she was unfazed.
She climbed up on the bench
as her papa bid her goodbye.

He rushed back home
to hear his daughter's public debut
as her audience would hear her—
on the radio.
He joined Sara, Frina,
and the rest of the family
crowding around.

In the broadcast studio,
the staff cued
Zhanna to begin.
And she did.
      Expertly.
          Until the unexpected happened.
After playing only eight bars,
a power outage struck.
The lights went out!
Zhanna sat in pitch blackness,
but she was still on the air.

> *There was no time to think. I had to keep*
> *playing even though I could not see my*
> *hands on the keyboard.*

Zhanna's papa's training
had served her well.

Despite being unable to see
the sheet music, her fingers, or the keys,
Zhanna's notes sparked in the dark
and lit up the airwaves.
Her first performance was a triumph!

It would not be her last.

STRUGGLING

Happy times
for Zhanna and her family
were swallowed up
when a power-hungry dictator
named Josef Vissarionovich Dzhugashvili
started to devour their country in the early 1930s.
He was better known as Joseph Stalin,
an alias he assumed meaning "Man of Steel."
Stalin had a plan for ridding the country
of the old ways and looking to the future.

FIVE-YEAR PLAN

Stalin
had a grand plan.
What cost to modernize?
Socialize? Industrialize?
Souls. Lives.

DEATH BY HUNGER

Stalin had seized absolute control
of the government
the year Zhanna was born.
Now little Zhanna heard talk of "taxes,"
"peasant uprisings,"
"hunger" and "famine"
when her parents thought
she wasn't listening.
Her worried grandparents
spoke quietly in Yiddish,
knowing she wouldn't understand.
Her family tried to keep
the terrible news from her,
but Zhanna saw with her own eyes
the effects of the Holodomor—
"death by hunger."
It didn't make sense.
Zhanna's Ukraine had so much food,
so many wheat farms,
it had been nicknamed
the "breadbasket of Europe."
Now her people were starving to death
thanks to the "Man of Steel"
and his Five-Year Plan.

"For the greater good,"
he pushed farmers off their own land
and made them work for state farms.
He sold their grain to other countries to buy
heavy industrial factory equipment,
while his own Soviet families were left to eat
field mice and bark from the trees.

Farmers fought back with axes and shotguns.
Stalin declared them enemies of the state
and ordered the secret police
to send them away to Siberia.
Fifty thousand farm families!

Zhanna saw beggars on the streets
of Berdyansk dying of hunger and the cold.

*I found two little girls in a hut close to the
hospital I used to visit. They had no bed,
no parents. I ran home and told my mother
that I had to take food to those children.
She gave me some, but I knew they had no
chance to survive.*

HARD TIMES

People had no money to buy bread,
let alone candies,
so Dmitri's business fell to pieces.
He struggled to pay Stalin's high taxes.

And there was a bigger problem.
Dmitri had never joined the Communist Party.
The authorities considered him a traitor.
And traitors were not tolerated.
They were terrorized.
>Or worse—
>they were killed.

S FOR SLAUGHTERED BY STALIN

Artists
Bankers
Chemists
Doctors
Engineers
Farmers
Garbage collectors
Historians
Intellectuals
Journalists
Kitchen workers
Lawyers
Minorities
Nurses
Officers
Police
Quarry workers
Religious leaders
Spies
Truck drivers
University professors
Veterans
Writers
X-ray technicians

Yeomen
Zoologists
    M for Millions Murdered.
     A for Anyone
       who would defy Stalin's rule.

WHAT GOES AROUND COMES AROUND

power was everything to Stalin
why was he so cruel?
is there any doubt
human life meant nothing to him
he was a murderer
he was a tyrant
was there a reason
to be exiled
to be injured
to be scarred
to be bullied
to be beaten
to be hungry
to be poor
he knew what it was
even as a boy
power was everything to Stalin

(Now read the poem from the bottom up.)

ARRESTED

Zhanna's papa was arrested by Stalin's men,
jailed, interrogated, and released,
over and over again.
Eight-year-old Zhanna took it upon herself
to wait on the street corner
watching for the secret police
so she could warn her papa.

> *I would run in the house and think,*
> *"Where am I going to hide my father?" The*
> *house was so small. I could only think of*
> *one place—but he was too big to hide in the*
> *basket of dirty laundry like Frina.*

One policeman burst into their house.

> *He said to my father, "You are Jewish—*
> *you've got to be rich. Where is the gold?" Of*
> *course, we didn't have any. He would show*
> *his pocket watch, but they had no interest*
> *in it. They wanted money—gold. They*
> *took Father away so many times.*

Zhanna's papa always came home,
but they all knew their luck was running out.

THEY'RE COMING

Time was up.
Dmitri could no longer pay his bills,
so the tax collectors informed him
they were coming to take
the family's furniture.

> *That was the last straw that broke us. I*
> *panicked at the fear of being homeless and*
> *I secretly cried—I didn't want my parents*
> *to see. We knew we had to leave before they*
> *took everything. They could have the rest,*
> *but my father was determined to save the*
> *piano and violin.*

Zhanna was eight years old
and Frina was six
when they said goodbye
to their childhood home
and to their grandparents,
who would manage on savings
and hope to join them later.
Zhanna left her beloved Berdyansk,
her candy-coated life,
on a coal-fired train with her parents,

her little sister,
a violin,
a small piano,
and not much else.

A NEW BEGINNING—1935

Zhanna and her family
made their new home
250 miles north, in Kharkov,
the former capital of Ukraine.
Over the years it had grown
into a vibrant Jewish center
with Hebrew publishers,
politicians, and professionals.
Zhanna and Frina's cousins
Tamara and Celia lived there.
Yet, moving to Katsarskaya Street,
in a city of nearly one million people,
was a far cry from small, scenic Berdyansk.
The Arshanskys' home was not a house,
but one room
in a run-down apartment building.

There were two small beds.
A couch.
Dresser.
Table.
Chairs.
Wood-burning stove.
The piano.

The bathroom,
down the hall,
was shared by
seven apartments.

Their only money
came from Dmitri
giving piano lessons
or playing violin
at occasional local concerts.
Meals were meager—
bread with a smear of sunflower oil.

CITY OF SIGHTS

Curious Zhanna explored the neighborhoods,
just as she had in Berdyansk.
She couldn't help but notice
the impressive Kharkov Choral Synagogue,
a domed architectural marvel,
one of the largest in Europe.
In a sign of the times,
the Soviets had shut it down
as a place of worship
and turned it into a Communist center
and sports complex.
Yes, change was afoot.
Still, as Zhanna walked to school,
she was entranced by
her new city of sights—
buses, trolleys, a circus,
theaters dating from the 1700s,
and an elaborate building
bolstered by ornate pillars—
the famed Kharkov Conservatory of Music.

HIGH HOPES

Despite their abysmal circumstances,
Dmitri still had sky-high hopes
for his daughters.
One day, he accompanied
eight-year-old Zhanna
and six-year-old Frina
to the renowned conservatory.

They would audition, and
the stakes couldn't have been higher.
This was their chance
to learn from the best,
to study music literature,
theory,
ensemble,
and chamber music.
They could never afford the school,
so this was the audition of their lives—
they needed two spots in the school
and two scholarships.

They entered
the majestic music school.
Each step up the wide staircase

was a reminder of just how high
they were trying to climb.
Portraits of the Russian giants of music
peered down their noses at them
with eyes that seemed to follow
their every move.
Upstairs awaited
a piano
and a long table
of stern-faced faculty.

Zhanna played first.

> *We had to play Bach. I also played a*
> *prelude from Bach's Clavier and a fugue in*
> *another key. Bach is God in Russia. If you*
> *don't know Bach, you don't know music.*

When Zhanna finished,
it was Frina's turn.
At the end, there was no applause.
The hush fell like a hammer.
Then the judges huddled together, whispering.
They were so serious
Zhanna was sure they had failed.

On the contrary,
they had nailed it.
The chairman approached their father
with hearty congratulations and
an offer to accept the girls on
scholarships, paying each of them
two hundred rubles per month.
They were *in,*
at ages eight and six,
the youngest children
ever awarded scholarships!
Two hundred rubles each!
Together, 400 rubles per month
was enough to support the girls
and their parents!

Best of all, they would be taught
by one of the most revered teachers
at the school—Abram Lvovsich Luntz,
a professor who had never taken
children as students.
He chose Zhanna and Frina
to be his first.

FOR THE LOVE OF CHOPIN

Professor Luntz introduced Zhanna
to what was to become her signature piece,
her favorite composition—
Chopin's *Fantaisie-Impromptu*.
She became obsessed.

> *I couldn't stop practicing it. The creation is so*
> *perfect, so spontaneous. . . . Chopin's ability*
> *to create the most gorgeous melodies in fast*
> *speed, with quick notes, staggered me. When*
> *Professor Luntz approved [my playing], I felt*
> *that I had become a grown-up.*

The sheet music
became Zhanna's most prized possession.

And soon, her only possession.

ON FIRE

As the girls' talent soared,
so did their reputation.
They were flying high until one day
scarlet fever, like a fiery arrow,
took Frina down.
Although antibiotics
had just been invented,
they were not widely available.
Children suffered high fevers,
sore throats, red sandpapery rashes,
and peeling skin.
Just like the boy in *The Velveteen Rabbit*,
patients had to be quarantined and
their belongings burned.
Thousands of children died before the 1940s,
just like Beth March in *Little Women*.

For Frina, this was no storybook fiction.
The first grader was hospitalized for months.
Her mother sat by her side every day.

It was a vicious thing. She was near death.

Then the infection spread
to her middle ear—
the part of the ear that transmits sound—
serious for anyone,
disastrous for a musician.

The doctors had heard Frina in concert.
They knew what was at stake for her
and decided to operate.
They took out a piece of bone
behind her ear,
with unintended results.

> *It left her with unequal hearing and*
> *balance.*

But the operation helped Frina recuperate.

> *[The doctors] treated her like their own*
> *daughter. Frina adored them. It helped her*
> *get well.*

It took months, but Frina recovered,
returned home,
and went back to school with her sister.

SCALING THE HEIGHTS

The girls' talents grew,
playing with giants
of the musical world.
Regina Horowitz, sister to Vladimir—
one of the greatest pianists of the century—
taught the girls once a week.

The trick was not only playing
the right notes
in the right order
at the right speed.
It was learning how to interpret a piece,
feeling the emotions behind it
and projecting them to the audience,
telling a story without words
using only touch and sound.

Front-row seats
to visiting luminaries' performances
taught the girls to hear
and recognize expert technique.
For Zhanna,
seeing a renowned young pianist play

was like seeing electric lights for the first
time. . . . Rosa Tamarkina brought out
the glory of [Chopin's] F-minor Concerto
for me. Tears of happiness were pouring
out of my eyes—it stamped Chopin in my
musical heart forever.

Watching backstage as
pianist Victor Topilin
played Mendelssohn's Concerto in E Minor
awakened a reverence for what the piano can do.

[He] brought out every bit of spirit that
Mendelssohn put into the piece. It is
enough to melt a stone. I sensed something
precious coming out of the piano which I
never forgot.

Still, Zhanna thought no one
could play Mozart
as her sister did.

Frina played the D-minor concerto with
fluent technique, but that's not why
everyone cried when she played it. She
grasped the spirit of the piece, the style.

Her [technique] was already developed
to a mature state, although the rest of her
was a child who played with dolls every
free moment.

The school recognized
that Zhanna's and Frina's talents
towered over other students'.
Their teachers paired the girls on the piano,
playing pieces for four hands—
Zhanna on the left playing bass,
Frina on the right playing treble.
Side by side on the piano bench,
the two very different sisters
came together as one.
For Zhanna, Frina was a baby no more.
She was a partner.
And an impressive one at that!

STAGE DEBUT

Soon the girls were ready
for their first concert.
But they couldn't afford new dresses.
The girls' professors,
who loved them like family,
stepped in to help.
Professor Luntz provided fabric
for matching sapphire-blue silk dresses
dotted with tiny snowflakes.
Each was tied with a smart sash belt
made of the same material.
They appeared on stage, polished and ready,
but their elegant attire paled beside
the beauty of their performance.

Their concert debut
was a resounding success,
reported in the newspapers,
and followed by a flurry
of other opportunities.
The sisters' talent snowballed,
and soon they were traveling to
Leningrad, Kiev, and beyond,
taking the competition by storm.

"LIFE IS GETTING MERRIER"

So said Stalin,
and his citizens spread the word
every time they sang the country's anthem.
It was all a lie, and yet . . .
When Zhanna was twelve and Frina was ten,
life did indeed seem to be getting better.

In 1939, Stalin made a deal
with another dictator—Germany's Hitler.
The two bullies agreed
that their countries would not attack each other
for the next ten years.
The people rejoiced
and business flourished!
Zhanna's grandparents were able to move
to an apartment in Kharkov
and open a sweets shop.

> *It was an absolute joy to have our*
> *grandparents back in our lives. We walked*
> *into their shop and knew we would get the*
> *most marvelous cakes with apples inside.*

Oh, to have their family together again!

There would be peace.
Free-flowing desserts
were the icing on the cake.
Life was getting better, comrades.

MERRIER STILL

The girls continued to compete
on the concert stage.
One competition led to another
and another, and finally to the top—
the Moscow State Conservatory.

Both girls played Bach on a golden piano
and each received a prize of her choice.
Zhanna chose a fountain pen;
Frina, a doll. Of course.
They were asked to return
for a private audition with
a professor at the pinnacle of his career—
Alexander Borisovich Goldenweiser.
A classmate of legendary composer
and pianist Rachmaninoff,
Goldenweiser had been a friend and
frequent house guest of the Russian author
of *War and Peace*, Leo Tolstoy.

> *He had the whole world waiting to*
> *study with him. Nobody was higher than*
> *Goldenweiser.*

The audition was held
in Goldenweiser's apartment.
Zhanna wondered if her talent
could measure up.
But she felt calm.

> *I am never nervous playing before true*
> *musicians, only the public. I played a Bach*
> *partita. I remember how profoundly he*
> *was listening.*

When she was finished,
he simply nodded at Frina to play.
Again, he listened,
silently,
intently.
She finished.
Again, silence.

Finally, he spoke.
He agreed to accept them!
He would provide each with a
100-ruble-a-month scholarship.
It was less than their current scholarship in Kharkov,
but to Zhanna the money didn't matter.

*I just got accepted by the most celebrated
piano teacher in the country!*

For Zhanna and Frina,
life was getting merrier,
a life with promise,
a life with a glorious future
       had just begun.

THE HARD TRUTH

Sadly, money did matter.
Zhanna's family could barely afford
to live in Kharkov
on 400 rubles a month.
Rents in Moscow were much more expensive.
How could they survive on 200 rubles,
half of what they had been earning?
            They couldn't.
They would have to turn down
the most celebrated teacher in the country,
continue with their music classes in Kharkov,
and go to school like everyone else.

Ho-hum. Zhanna was just as bored
at her neighborhood school
as she had been in kindergarten.
Whatever School 13 had to teach her
had nothing to do with her life
as a musician.

The only upside
was her social life,
with a new best friend—
Irina Vlodavskaya.
The two thirteen-year-olds
were opposites in many ways,
Irina shy,
Zhanna a whirlwind.
But they complemented each other.
Irina recalled Zhanna as
"slim as a young birch tree"
with long chestnut curls
and big gray eyes.
"Never in my life
had I seen eyes beaming
with such joy of life
and friendliness."

Zhanna was openhearted,
not at all like the other girls
at school.

They gave each other nicknames:
Zhanna became "Zhaba"—frog
because of her large eyes.
Irina became "Psina"—doggie,
a nod to her love of pooches.

Irina spent many hours listening
to Zhanna and Frina play piano at home
and proudly attended their concerts.
Irina thought her friends
were "wunderkinds,"
and was surprised
that "even the noisiest success"
couldn't "spoil these prodigies.
They never showed
even a shadow of conceit."

War was raging across Europe,
but thanks to Stalin's misguided trust in Hitler,
life was merry for Zhanna and her friends
—filled with movies, concerts, good books,
girlhood secrets, and giggles.

Then one morning started the beginning of
the end of that life.

Zhanna and her dad
went out for a Sunday morning's excursion,
shopping and strolling the streets together
like the pals they were.
They stopped for ice cream,
sitting beneath the statue
of the national poet of Ukraine,
Taras Shevchenko.
Suddenly the public radio speakers
on the streets blared with an
official announcement:

"Citizens of the Soviet Union!
The Soviet government
and its head, Comrade Stalin,
have instructed me to make the
following announcement:
Today, at four a.m. . . .
German troops attacked our country . . ."

The shocking news hit the people broadside.
Hitler's attack was a gut punch,
taking their breath away.
Their country had been at peace with Germany
for two years,
only a fraction of the ten years Stalin and Hitler
had promised in their nonaggression pact.
The two countries had made a deal,
but Hitler was a smiling bully,
like a gangster who
uses one hand to shake on a deal,
and hides a knife
behind his back with the other.

Hitler had turned on Stalin,
his professed ally,
in a surprise invasion
code-named Operation Barbarossa.
In the predawn hours, while Stalin slept,
Hitler sent more than 3.5 million soldiers
marching into the Soviet Union,
with more than 3,400 tanks
and 2,700 aircraft.

Why the betrayal?
Conquering Russia had always been

a special obsession for Hitler.
After taking over western Europe,
he schemed a way to turn east,
to seize his "friend's" rich farmland,
giving more "living space" to Germans,
while ridding the world
of Slavs, Jews, Bolsheviks,
and others Hitler considered "vermin."
He would uproot the Slavic history
and culture he despised
to allow German civilization
to bloom and spread.

Now the attack was underway.
Would Hitler's troops reach Kharkov?

Feeling lost and confused,
Zhanna and her papa ran home
to warn their family.

> *Everyone [was] crying in the streets.*

WHO WAS WORSE? HITLER OR STALIN?

As the Germans advanced,
some Russians who had suffered
under Stalin welcomed Hitler,
hailing him a liberator.
They greeted Nazi soldiers
with gifts of bread, salt, and flowers.
Some took up weapons
and became Nazi collaborators
against their fellow citizens.
Shifting alliances swept the country
as confusion and chaos
paved the way for destruction.

THE SUMMER OF BOMBS

Things would only get worse.

> *Kharkov was one of the bombing targets*
> *of the Germans almost right away. They*
> *succeeded in making ruins of about three-*
> *fourths of this cultured, musical city.*

Air-raid sirens pierced the night
with their ghostly wails,
but there were no shelters to run to.
Zhanna's papa helped to dig ditches
and cover them with boards
where people cowered
"like cockroaches,"
said Zhanna's friend Irina.
School 13 was transformed
into a refugee center
for those whose homes
had been destroyed.
One day, a bomb
tore the walls from a house
one block from school.
Zhanna and her family
sought underground shelter.

We had to walk to some basement of a tall building each night and sleep without any bedding. I considered it torture.

Things would only get worse. . . .

SCORCHED EARTH

Stalin ordered the Red Army to
"fight to the last drop of blood,"
but the Germans kept coming.
In retreat, Stalin demanded
his armies leave nothing
but destruction in their wake.
"The enemy must not be left
a single engine, a single railway truck,
not a single pound of grain
or gallon of fuel."
He ordered guerrilla units to
"blow up bridges and roads,
damage telephone and telegraph lines,
set fire to forests, stores, and transports."
Caught between Hitler's advancing Wehrmacht
and Stalin's "scorched earth,"
people knew they had to get out.

FLIGHT

Many fled,
people of all faiths;
fear had no religion.
So many evacuated,
so many died,
that Kharkov,
a city of 1.5 million,
counted fewer than 200,000 souls
two years later.

Many fled
in the summer and fall of 1941,
including more than 100,000
of Kharkov's 130,000 Jews.
People escaped any way they could,
even crammed onto cattle cars,
heading east to the Ural Mountains
and Siberia, dodging Hitler's grasp.

Many fled,
including Zhanna's cousins Tamara and Celia,
and her aunt and uncle.
They were headed east,
as far from the Germans as possible.

They begged Zhanna's mother to come
or at least send the girls.
Her mother Sara couldn't believe
that the Germans would harm them,
and she wasn't strong enough to make the trip.
Sara had been a swimmer when she was young,
but childbirth had weakened her heart.
She also suffered from terrible asthma.
They had no choice.
Zhanna's family had to stay
and wait it out.

> *We never dreamed we would be killed.*
> *We thought . . . the Germans would send us*
> *to a work camp, they would be kicked out,*
> *and we would be home again.*

Many fled,
including Irina,
Zhanna's best friend from School 13,
the one she called "Psina" or "Ino."
The girls met at the train station
to say a tearful goodbye,
Zhanna handing her friend
a postcard from her and Frina.

It showed two musicians on the front. On the back, it read,

> *Well, Ino, if you ever forget me, then*
> *watch out! Wishing you happiness in*
> *everything you do. So long from me*
> *forever. Please never forget me.*
> *Love, Zhaba and Puzha.*
> *Kharkov—15.09.41*

WHAT WAS COMING

Zhanna couldn't have known
what was coming.
Stalin had blocked news of Hitler's crimes
when they were allies.
People had heard
vague rumors of work camps,
but few knew of the murders
in Germany and Poland.

> *Stalin was guilty, a . . . criminal not to*
> *alert Jews to slaughters in the west. If*
> *Stalin had said one word, confirming the*
> *rumors, we would have crawled to get out.*

Few knew that the *Einsatzgruppen*,
the Germans' mobile killing squads,
were coming.
These soldiers had one mission:
to murder "undesirables"—
Communists, Soviet officials,
Roma, people with disabilities,
and above all else . . . Jewish people.
It was the start of Hitler's "Final Solution."
By the end of that year,

at least half a million Ukrainian Jews
(some say three times that number)
would be killed,
at least 16,000 of them from Kharkov.

ELEGY

The *Einsatzgruppen*
rolled into the Soviet Union
following orders to eliminate
an entire population:
round them up,
march them to a ravine,
line them up,
and shoot.
Murder most foul
and cowardly.
September 29, 1941
Babi Yar
nearly 34,000 Jewish men,
women,
and yes,
children.
Gone.
And the mobile killing squads in Kiev
rolled on.

They were coming for Kharkov next.

SILENCE

Zhanna's explorer days were over.
She and her family cowered inside.
They couldn't play piano
for fear the sound might attract attention.
All music stopped,
the way some birds go silent
in the still air before a storm.

THE FALL

The Nazi storm swept into Kharkov
at the end of October.
And the people,
helpless to hold on to their lives,
found themselves in free fall,
torn from their roots.

Their city came crashing down.

SHAKEDOWN

It wasn't long before
they came for Zhanna's family.

> *They came to our room because they were*
> *looking for Jews and someone told them*
> *where we were living.*

First was a single Nazi officer
who barged in
late one night, demanding gold.
They told the truth.
They had none.
The officer spat and
screamed that they were liars.
Then he spotted Dmitri's violin.

> *We caught our breath and begged him not*
> *to take it. It was a knife in our hearts. He*
> *took it.*

A few nights later
two German soldiers
arrived looking
to pillage the apartment.

They tried to take the piano,
but couldn't manage it.
One held Dmitri's hands behind his back.
The other slammed Sara against the wall
and held a pistol to her head,
while the girls wailed hysterically.
Eventually, the soldiers left empty-handed
realizing what the family said was true—
there were no treasures to be had.

> *That was the beginning of true terror.*
> *After my father's violin was gone and they*
> *attacked our mother, we knew anything*
> *could happen to us.*

TRUE TERROR

Tragedies hang in the city trees
We're all at the end of our ropes.
The Nazis make sure everyone sees
tragedies hang in the city trees—
dead bodies twist in the chilling breeze,
choking our prayers and our hopes.
Tragedies hang in the city trees
We're all at the end of our ropes.

THE REAPER

More than 100 people were hanged
in the square in the first two weeks.
Zhanna saw some strung from the
statue of the poet laureate
Taras Shevchenko.
His face was frozen in stone,
but the words of his poems still echoed
the history of pain in Ukraine:
All the night the reaper reaps
Never stays his hands nor sleeps,
Reaping endlessly.
Wouldst thou hide in field or town?
Where thou art, there he will come;
He will reap thee down.

THE REAPER ROAMS THE WORLD

It was that December
when the reaper's hand reached
across the oceans to those who thought
they could stay out of the war,
stay safe.

It was that December
that the reaper came for America.
As Zhanna and her family cowered
in their apartment in Kharkov,
Germany's ally, Japan,
blew up American ships
docked at Pearl Harbor in Hawaii.

It was that December,
December 7, 1941,
that more than 2,000 sailors died
and the United States dove into the fight.

It was that December,
that American families woke up
knowing what it was like
to have their country,
their homes attacked.

They knew a little more
what it was like
to be the families of Europe.
To be Zhanna.

THE KHARKOV COUNT BEGINS

Thousands of miles
across the seas from Pearl Harbor,
the countdown to disaster in Kharkov
began with the Nazis dividing Jews,
adding them to lists,
aided by local officials and collaborators.
Zhanna's mother heard
that proof of baptism
could absolve residents,
scrub them from the Nazis' list—
their terrible "yellow papers."
Sick as she was with her asthma
and heart condition,
Sara walked through town
searching for a priest
who would change her family
into Christians.
Zhanna went with her.

> *The one Russian Orthodox priest we got to*
> *see refused to do the baptism.*

That "no" slammed the door
on any way out.

Their names were on the Nazis' list.

On December 14, 1941,
decrees posted throughout the city
ordered all Jews to report
to the center of town
and prepare for evacuation
the following day.
Zhanna's parents sold
their few household items
to buy a sled
that would carry their clothing and bedding.
Their beloved piano had to stay behind.
If they did not prepare to go,
if they did not report,
they would be shot on the spot.

SAYING GOODBYE

Later that day,
Zhanna rushed to say goodbye
to a good friend from School 13—
Svetlana Gaponovitch.
She gave her friend
her sapphire-blue concert dress
with its matching sash belt for safekeeping
and promised she would come back for it.
She also gave her friend a photo of herself with Frina.
On the back, it said,

To Dear Svetulya from Zhanna!

Sveta,
You know at what kind of moment I'm giving you
this picture. I don't know if we will ever see each
other again. Take care. Remember your two dear
friends Zhanna and Frina.

Kharkov, 14.XII.41
sad/sorrowful year

Zhanna left Svetlana's house
wondering if she would ever
see her friend again.

DECEMBER 15, 1941

It was time.
At noon,
Zhanna's family and the others
gathered at the end of their street
in bone-chilling cold,
just 5°F above zero.

> *The Germans were taking pictures and*
> *laughing at us. That was very painful.*

Snow, icy as the officers' stares,
blanketed the ground,
whitewashing the terrible proceedings.
Where were they going?
Nobody knew.

> *We were told, and we were hoping, that*
> *we were being sent to work. We were*
> *willing to work. The conversation was*
> *that they had some camps. We didn't*
> *understand. We weren't criminals. We*
> *were citizens, very lawful citizens.*

Zhanna,
Frina,
their parents,
and their grandparents
joined the 16,000 other Jews
trudging to the designated factory.
They moved slowly under bulky winter coats,
each with a bit of fish or bread,
small souvenirs of the lives they led,
hearts and heads filled with dread.

Suddenly, Zhanna stopped,
insisting she had to go back.
She had forgotten something.
Before her parents could protest,
before the guards could notice,
she turned and ran.
Her papa called after her
under his breath,
desperate to stop her,
desperate that she wouldn't be shot.
       She was gone.

A RISKY RUN

Zhanna ran and ran,
cutting through the crowds,
who were astonished to see this child in flight.
   She dodged
       and
     weaved
       the four blocks back home,
   and ran inside.
She rushed to her beloved piano
standing all alone in the disarray,
forlorn and abandoned.
Zhanna pushed the piano's
stacks of sheet music aside
in her frantic search.
The works of the great German composers—
Bach, Schumann, Handel—
the gods of music to Zhanna's family
fluttered to the ground
like fallen angels.

There!
She found what she was looking for—
the music for Chopin's *Fantaisie-Impromptu*.
It was her favorite piece,

the one her teacher had given her,
the one she couldn't leave behind.
Not ever.
She needed *Fantaisie-Impromptu*
now that fate had become all too real.

With Chopin's music
tucked inside her shirt, by her heart,
she was ready to face whatever lay ahead.
But she had to get back to her family.

THE MARCHERS MARCHED ON

Zhanna ran back
and found her family again,
to their gasping relief.
Together, they slogged through the snow
in a bone-weary procession
so similar to
the mournful funeral processions
Zhanna used to follow as a child,
except this time there was no music.
Unlike other mourners,
these men, women, children
still had no idea what lay ahead.
Where were they going?
What would happen to them?

Other people lined the streets
mostly watching in silence,
but some called out, laughing,
and hectoring the doomed souls.
Hitler had claimed
Jews were to blame for the war
and some believed him.
Flames of hostility and prejudice flared,
fed by hatred for some, by fear for others.

In flyers posted around town,
the Nazis had made it clear
that anyone helping a Jew would be shot.
The penalty for human kindness
was your life
and the lives of your entire family.
The marchers marched on.
Children stumbled.
      The elderly crumpled.
        The cold closed in.
But with fear of the firing squad
suffocating sympathy,
even the kindest onlookers
stared with eyes of steel
and hearts hardened to stone.

NIGHTFALL

It was more than eight miles
to their destination,
an abandoned tractor factory,
and by nightfall,
they still had miles to go.
Worse, Zhanna's grandparents
had disappeared, lost in the crowd.
Dmitri searched frantically for them,
but there were too many people
and it was getting dark.
The temperature dropped and
the wicked wind
whipped through their clothes.
People collapsed in the snow.
Dmitri couldn't find his parents,
but he did find
a tiny three-sided shed
where the rest of his family
might find shelter.

> *The wind hit us, but not as hard. Only three*
> *of us could fit inside, in a standing position,*
> *so all night we took turns, one of us standing*
> *outside. We did not know if [my mother]*
> *could survive the night.*

AWAKENED

Daybreak uncovers
what dark's mercy had tucked in.
Snowy mounds. Corpses.

GOOD NEWS, BAD NEWS

The good news was that
Zhanna's mother was alive.
Her family had survived.
There were her grandparents!
They were all together again.

The bad news was that
the guards were back.
Their guns were armed.
The marchers marched on.

THE BARRACKS

Zhanna's new home
for the next two weeks
was the empty tractor factory—
long rows of derelict housing,
27 one-story buildings,
each one meant for about 70 workers.
Now each *room*,
meant for six to eight people,
held 70 Jews crammed together.
Freezing winds
blew through the broken windows,
turning the cement floors to ice.
There were no bathrooms,
there was no food,
there was a long line for water.
Was this the labor camp
they had been told about?

People started dying that first day
from starvation, exhaustion,
humiliation, disease, and madness.
People were shot for no reason.
People who were too old or too young
were packed in trucks,
never to be seen again.

A shed with three holes in the ground
served as the women's "toilet,"
overflowing with sewage,
diarrhea, and filth.
Even the cold
couldn't smother the stench.

> *It was inhuman. The sight of women*
> *the age of my mother and grandmother*
> *made me shake in shame for the Germans.*

Rage at her captors
made Zhanna want to get away.
She went to scout out her surroundings,
despite barbed wire and gun-happy guards.
She discovered a trash heap
behind a small fence.

> *The fence was a little shorter than I was,*
> *but I didn't see any reason I could not use*
> *it for my bathroom. The Germans would*
> *probably shoot me if they saw me. Since*
> *fear was present every minute anyway, I*
> *decided to take the chance.*

Zhanna's mother had packed
a small food supply for her family,

mostly dried fish.
When it started to run out,
Zhanna knew what she had to do.

GOING HOME

At twilight before the searchlights
lit up the compound,
Zhanna crept along the barbed-wire fence
until she found a small opening
and squeezed through.

> *My parents couldn't stop me. I was like a*
> *pet returning to his home. I had to bring*
> *back food.*

She started walking back,
back to Kharkov.
It was such a long way—eight miles—
and night's shadows stalked her.
She felt weak after walking for two hours,
faint with hunger.
Up ahead she saw a house.
Would the people there help her?
    Or report her?
Either was possible.
She took a chance
and knocked on the door.

*They opened the door for me and asked no
questions. They just saw a cold kid. I said
I am walking to Kharkov and I have no
place to sleep. They allowed me in, gave me
something warm to eat, and put me in bed.*

The war was filled with
blessings and betrayals.
Zhanna was blessed that night.

KHARKOV

Zhanna arrived back
in her hometown the next day
and wandered the streets,
wondering how to find food.
Zhanna was a city celebrity,
famous for her concerts,
so she had to be careful
no one recognized her.
She couldn't buy food; she had no money.
She dug into the stinking garbage cans
at the end of her street,
finding potato peelings and other scraps.
She gathered as much as she could carry.
   And started the long walk
   back to her family.

The garbage was enough
to keep Zhanna's family alive
in the coming days.
She left the barracks twice,
sheltered by the same family
along the way each time.
The family never asked her name.
They never asked how or why
this young girl was so desperate,
so all alone.
They didn't want to know.
They simply took her in, fed her,
and gave her a warm bed.
Their kindness, if discovered,
could put them in grave danger.
They could all be killed.
But it was given freely.

Coming and going
from the tractor factory,
Zhanna was never caught.
Why didn't the guards notice her leaving?
Why wasn't she shot?
Zhanna was convinced the guards saw

and turned their heads.

No questions asked.

None needed.

They knew what was coming.

> *It was easier to end many lives in one*
> *operation where the ditches are ready. . . .*
> *It was not worth the bullets or the noise to*
> *shoot just one Jew.*

PYRAMID SCHEME

The
day after
Christmas,
Zhanna saw a
pile growing in the
snow. It was a stack
of sentimental family
keepsakes—beloved dolls,
teddy bears, framed photos, well-
loved books, eyeglasses, pipes, prayer
shawls, pocket watches—whatever had
been small enough and precious enough for
families to carry through the snow. Anything
valuable had been stolen by the soldiers long ago.

SECRET STASH

They wanted all of our possessions,
absolutely anything, all that we had. It
was growing and growing. Germans
were greedy, stingy, merciless. They took
everything they could.

But they didn't get everything.
Without telling anyone
and at great personal danger,
Zhanna held on to the one thing
she had from home—
her Chopin sheet music,
her *Fantaisie-Impromptu.*

And unbeknownst to anyone,
her papa hid his gold watch.

THE ROAD TO DOOM

The Nazis kept saying they were
taking their prisoners south to Poltava
to a labor camp.
But Zhanna's papa was from Poltava;
it was his hometown.
He knew his geography.
He noticed trucks loaded
with very young children headed
in the opposite direction,
away from Poltava.

> *When he saw the trucks go north, my papa*
> *knew they were going to kill us because*
> *there was nothing to the north. It was the*
> *road to nowhere.*

Zhanna's papa had his suspicions,
but no one knew for sure
that they were on their way
down a different road to doom.
They were soon to be herded
to a ravine about four miles southeast,
where they would find two enormous pits in the ground.
The ravine was soon to be a massive grave
called Drobitsky Yar.

THE LAST MARCH

It was shortly after Christmas
on a cut-crystal day—
glittering sunshine on snow—
that the Nazis rounded up
the last group of prisoners,
including Zhanna and her family,
to be marched the remaining miles
to Drobitsky Yar.

They sorted the people into
formal columns and rows,
interspersed with German
transport trucks.
Turncoat Ukrainian guards toting rifles
marched alongside,
followed by SS soldiers
with pistols and rubber whips.
Zhanna's family made one row across:

Grandpa, Grandma, Papa, Zhanna, Frina, and Mama

A young Ukrainian guard
not much older than Zhanna
marched beside them.

He was tall, young, nice-looking.

Zhanna's papa started speaking to him softly
in Ukrainian. Zhanna heard him say,
"Please let my little girl go."
He quietly gestured at her.
Dmitri knew that Zhanna alone
had a chance to survive
on her own in the woods.
But the guard didn't respond.
He kept marching.

How could Dmitri make this boy listen?
Ah! His watch!
It had a white porcelain face
with Roman numerals and a gold cover.
He dug deep into his pocket and
flashed the gold at the guard.
Would it tempt him?
Would it save his daughter's life?
Zhanna's papa asked the guard again
to let his little girl step out of line.

> *I was next to my papa, walking and
> listening. I thought, "That's what he wants
> me to do? Well, how am I going to do it?"*

A lot of other Jews heard what my papa was saying. They were as . . . tense about it as anybody. [They probably thought] if anybody can jump out [of the line], God bless them.

The guard glanced at the watch,
snatched it, and agreed.
He would look away.

ESCAPE

Dmitri nodded at Zhanna.
She understood.
She had to find a way out of line
without calling attention to herself
or her family.
        Or they could all be shot.

Just ahead by the side of the road,
she spotted barbed wire rolled up
on its side
next to two old peasant women
who were watching the procession.
Zhanna realized she could jump
into the center of the rolled wires
and pretend to be one of the onlookers,
caught in the wire.

At that moment,
Dmitri pulled off his heavy winter coat
and put it on Zhanna's shoulders.
He whispered, "I don't care what you do. Just live."

It was now or never.

THE OTHER SIDE

Zhanna leapt out of line
silent as a hare diving into his hole.
It had taken just a second—
a blink of an eye,
a turn of a head,
a beat of a breath,
a pound of a pulse.
The old peasant women had seen her jump
and were watching her now, petrified.
A German with a whip glared at her
for a few terrifying seconds . . .

and walked on.

The Ukrainian guard was already ahead.

Zhanna watched the procession pass.

I could feel the eyes and good wishes of many souls on their last march. It was like they were holding me up in the air above the danger so I would not be harmed. Our hearts were connected. I saw my mother and father looking back at me. I stood and watched that column a long time.

And I cried and cried and cried.

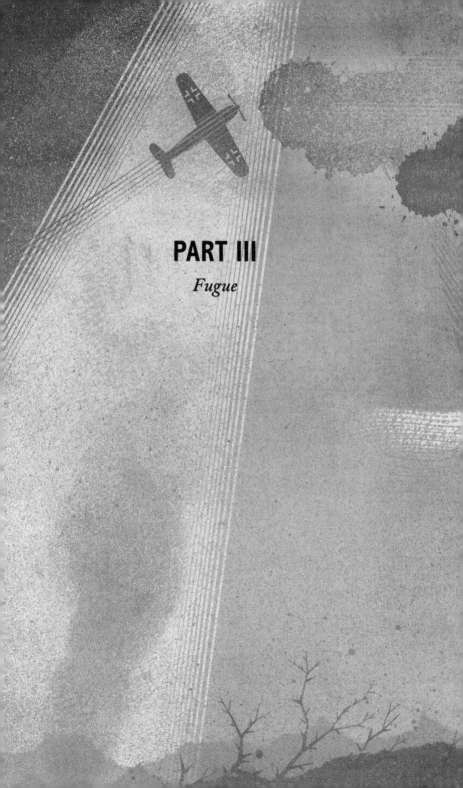

PART III

Fugue

TURNING AROUND

As the prisoners
were forced to march the remaining mile
toward their deaths,
Zhanna turned and walked
in the opposite direction,
tears streaming down her face,
urine freezing her clothes to her body,
toward Kharkov,
toward her old home,
toward the rest of her life.

PAIN

Tears rained down
staining her cheeks
straining her chest
draining her heart.

Tears rained down.
Who could explain
the insanity,
the inhumanity?

Tears rained down.
    Tears cried in vain.

SEEKING SHELTER

Zhanna stopped at the same house
on the way to Kharkov
where she was once again given shelter.
If they noticed her tears,
her papa's long coat,
they still knew not to ask questions.
They fed her and gave her a place to sleep.

The next day she continued on,
crying and walking,
crying and walking,
breathing in the scent of her papa
still on his coat,
covering her, embracing her,
remembering the sight of Frina
holding their mama's hand,
her little sister
who had just started to grow up,
the sister she was just starting to get to know.

WHO CAN HELP?

Back in Kharkov,
Zhanna needed more than food this time.
She needed help.
With her family gone,
she turned to her friends.

She would go back
to Svetlana Gaponovitch,
the friend she had visited
the day before the march.
Zhanna knew Svetlana's papa was Jewish.
He had moved away from their home earlier,
but Zhanna knew his family
would understand her plight.
Surely, they would help.
Zhanna knocked on the door.

Svetlana's mother opened the door a crack
and peeked out.
She saw Zhanna and . . .
understood all too well.
Wham!
The door slammed shut in her face,
the sound as painful as a crack in her chest.

Svetlana watched from a back window,
powerless to change her mother's mind.

Shattered, Zhanna stumbled off
as the frigid night
threatened to swallow her.
She walked farther,
keeping her head down,
dodging German police
who patrolled the streets.
What now?

She came to another classmate's house—
Lida Slipko's.
Her mother was rumored to be an anti-Semite,
but Zhanna was faint with hunger,
faint with the gaping hole in her heart.
She had no other choice.
She raised her hand to the door
and knocked.

Lida and her mother opened the door right away
        and pulled her inside.

To Zhanna, this turn of events
was a stunning thing.
> Sometimes people you've opened your heart to
> can fail you.
> Sometimes, compassion can be found
> where you least expect it.

KEEP MOVING

Zhanna knew she couldn't stay long
in any one place.
It was too dangerous
for the families who sheltered her.

Lida suggested the house of a boy
in their school.
Nicolai Bogancha and Zhanna
weren't friends, but acquaintances
who lived in the same neighborhood.
Zhanna approached the large house
of the older boy she admired
and knocked on the ten-foot-high gate.
The door opened.

> *I saw the loveliest and most welcoming
> figure saying to me, "I know who you are,"
> stretching her arm out to mine and pulling
> me inside.*

It was Nicolai's mother,
who recognized Zhanna
from the neighborhood
and from her many acclaimed performances.

Nicolai shyly said hello.
The Boganchas were well-to-do
with plenty of room, plenty of food.
They agreed to take care of her,
for a short time,
despite the danger to themselves.
If the Gestapo found Zhanna,
they knew the entire family could be killed.
She would be a secret.
But for now, she could rest.

> *It was such a heavenly thing to be in a place with people. One place. To be fed, to be safe.*

THE SECRET WAS OUT

Unfortunately,
people had seen Zhanna.
After all, she was a piano prodigy
who had been in the newspapers
after her many concerts.
Had Svetlana or Lida
told others they had seen her?
Had neighbors seen her
back on her old street?
Had someone noticed her
going into Nicolai's house?
       Someone had.

SHOCKING FACTS

Despite the Boganchas' efforts to hide her,
someone approached young Nicolai
with a shocking fact.
Nicolai's friend
knew Zhanna was hiding in their house,
and then whispered
a more shocking fact,
pointing out another house.
      Nicolai ran home to tell Zhanna.

STUNNING NEWS

It was heart-stopping,
fairy-tale, happy-ending news.
Great joy and a whirl of questions
filled the house that night.

Could it be true?
If so, when?
How?
Who else knew?
What could they do?
Was it safe?

So many questions, so many possibilities,
but nothing mattered more than this:

Frina was ALIVE!

RESCUE

In the dead of night,
without being asked,
Nicolai's papa slipped out of the house
into the shadows, wary of Nazis
who might be patrolling the streets.
He wasn't gone long.
When he returned,
he hurried in the door
with a gift for Zhanna.
      Her sister!
The girls fell into each other's arms.

What had happened?
  How had she escaped?
    What of their family?

Frina wouldn't answer.
She wouldn't speak of it.

Then
  or ever.

She was so bound up. The hurt was so big.

The girls wrapped their arms around each other,
grateful for these second chances
at life,
        and as sisters.

They silently agreed never to look back.
It was time to look forward
        to what lay ahead.

A PLAN

The sisters knew they had to get away.
They were too famous in Kharkov,
too many people knew their name,
knew they were Jewish.
Nicolai's parents
helped them devise a getaway plan—
new names,
   new ages,
      new lives.
They chose aliases
that would be easy to remember,
and a new life story:
they would pretend to be orphans.

Whether Zhanna knew it or not,
whether Frina would admit it or not,
after Drobitsky Yar they didn't need to pretend.
They were orphans indeed.

They practiced their story over and over again,
rehearsing how they would introduce themselves.

My name is Anna Morozova. I am from
Kharkov. My sister Marina and I are
orphans. Our father was an officer in the
Red Army and was killed in action. Our
mother died in the bombing of Kharkov.

They needed official identification papers
and could get them
IF
they were admitted to an orphanage.
But Zhanna was almost 15,
almost too old for an orphanage.

The solution? She changed her April 1 birthday
to December 25—that most Christian of holidays.
That way she could be 14 longer.
Frina changed her birthday too,
so she would still be two years younger.

They turned back the clock
        because they couldn't turn back time.

WHAT THEY LEFT BEHIND

One last thing before they left for good:
picking up things they left behind—
the sapphire silk dresses—
sneaking one last goodbye,
with love and regret
to Svetlana,
to childhood—
gone. So
long.

WHAT THEY DIDN'T KNOW

As the girls left Svetlana's house,
with their dresses,
one blue snowflake sash
dropped into the snow.
They walked on.
They didn't know.

Later, Svetlana found it
and tucked it away.
She kept it for nearly 80 years,
a sapphire-blue keepsake,
a remembrance
of two true friends
she had been powerless to save.
She put the silken sash away,
as she put away childish things.

The threads that bind,
the ties of friendship,
unspooled and snarled
in the tangle of war,
but did not break.

ON THE ROAD

Packing their blue concert dresses
and Chopin's *Fantaisie-Impromptu*,
Zhanna and Frina left the protection
of their benefactors
on the back of a horse-drawn cart.
The Boganchas had hired the driver
to take them to the edge of Kharkov.
From there, the plan was to walk
15 miles to Lubotin
and catch a train west to Poltava,
their papa's hometown.
Since the Germans were headed east,
in the opposite direction,
it seemed like a good plan.

They jumped down from the horse cart at noon
and followed the train tracks west,
walking for hours until the sun set.
The temperature dropped.
The Russian snows fell heavy
on their heads, shoulders, and eyelashes
weighing them down,
adding to their considerable burdens,
slowing their steps.

Mother Russia and Mother Nature
showed cruel indifference to two little girls
trying to put one foot in front of the other
with no boots,
no money,
little food.
Where would they go that night?
Soon it was dark.
Pitch dark.

To Zhanna's horror,
Frina lay down in the snow
            and refused to get up.

GIVING UP

Frina was broken—
frozen from head to toe,
hungry to her core,
dead on her feet.
She didn't want to go on anymore.
The little girl who liked to stay home,
play with her dolls,
and cuddle with her mama,
no longer had her home,
her dolls,
or her mama.
All she had was her sister,
who knew Frina would freeze to death
if she went to sleep in the snow.
Frina wouldn't listen to Zhanna's pleas.
She just wanted to be left alone.

FALLING

Frina was stubborn,
but Zhanna kept trying to reason with her.

> *I wasn't going to leave her in the snow. I
> said, "You have to get up and I will help
> you."*

Zhanna begged Frina
to think of a better life ahead,
to think of the sister she would leave all alone,
to think of the memory of their parents.

Nothing. No sound, no response.

The snow kept
       f
           a
              l
                  l
                      i
                          n
                             g. . . .

Zhanna had one last thing to say.
If Frina didn't get up,
she would lie down too.

Frina got up.

THE KINDNESS OF STRANGERS

Zhanna and Frina survived
that frightful, frozen night,
thanks to warm souls and an open door
in the tiny village of Lubotin.

> *We were asked in and were allowed to sleep*
> *on the stone floor in the entry. There was*
> *barely enough room to stretch our legs, but*
> *we slept like the stones under us.*

THE CATTLE CAR

Leaving at dawn,
the girls walked to the train station.
With no money for a ticket,
they found an empty cattle car
at the back of the train
and sneaked aboard.
There was no heat and no toilet,
the car empty except for old straw,
smelling earthy and musty.

A few others clambered aboard,
glancing at the girls in the corner,
but no one bothered them.
Leaving at noon, they traveled
hours and hours.
Zhanna and Frina leaned back, closed their eyes,
hypnotized by the rocking, rumbling rhythm
of the train,
echoing the rumbling
of their empty stomachs.

WHAT YOU WILL DO WHEN YOU'RE HUNGRY

The train pulled into Poltava that evening.
The girls climbed down
from the cattle car
and entered the station.
They squeezed onto a bench
in the waiting room
packed with people.
Ravenous, they watched a woman
feed bits of food to a tiny dog.
They watched a man
who pulled off his boots
and unwrapped the filthy rags
wound around his feet.
He worked with great concentration
to pick the dirt out
from between each toe.
Zhanna and Frina
watched with disgust and fascination
as he put his grimy boots back on
and then reached into his bag
for a piece of bread,
touching it with the same fingers
that had picked those toes.

All I could think of was his hands and
what they had been handling. We were
out of bread, out of everything. We were
starving to death.

So when the man extended
his grubby hands to the girls,
offering to share,
Zhanna and Frina took the bread.
And gobbled it up.

THE BRIDGE

With the morning's sun
rose a new challenge.
The girls had to find an orphanage.
It was the only place
that could issue them official papers
to validate their made-up names and ages.
Without those papers,
they could be detained by Nazis at any time.

But to get into downtown Poltava,
they had to cross a bridge.
Without papers.
A bridge heavily guarded
by Nazis checking IDs,
Nazis on the lookout for Jews.

CROSSING

As the girls walked,
they hoped for a crowd
crossing the bridge—
a throng of early morning townspeople.
so they could blend in.

There was no one.
Zhanna and Frina
turned up their coat collars
to hide their faces
as one of two Nazis holding a rifle
approached and blocked their path.

> *We were terrified. We had to try our story
> about Anna and Marina. We had practiced
> it many times, but this was the first
> performance. My heart was in my feet.
> "My name is Anna Morozova. . . ."*

Zhanna didn't get far with her story
before the guard stopped her.
He peered at them closely,
pulling their collars aside
to see their faces.

They waited while he studied them
and held their breath
as he turned to his partner.
Did he know they were lying?

"Sie sind Kinder!" he told his partner.
These are children.
"Geht!" he said,
and motioned for the girls to go on.
        In the breath of a sigh, they were across.

OPENING DOORS, CLOSING DOORS

Exhausted, once again the girls
knocked on doors in Poltava,
relying on the kindness of strangers
for short-term stays.

They were in and out,
up and down,
still essentially homeless,
rootless.

Zhanna met a lovely Russian professor
named Oleg Stepanovich,
who worked as a translator
for the Nazi commandant in Poltava.
He was a widower,
an elegant intellectual
who lived with an elderly woman,
who had been his childhood nanny.
She had cared for him,
so now he was looking after her.
Oleg offered Zhanna shelter in return
for helping him care for the woman
while he was at work.
He had a small home,

stuffed with books.
There was room for only Zhanna.
For Frina, he found a family
of two teachers.
They opened their home to her,
but what went on behind closed doors
was another story.

> *They were heartless and cruel. They kept*
> *Frina starving and working like a slave.*
> *I saved little pieces of bread to take to her.*
> *It broke my heart because my place was*
> *terrific.*

The situation was far from ideal,
but they didn't have much choice.
Then one day, two months later,
something awful happened.

Zhanna was recognized.

"YOU'RE ALIVE!"

Starving refugees
from the girls' old city of Kharkov
started pouring into Poltava
looking for food, for grain.

> *I was walking down the street in*
> *Poltava and saw people I knew from the*
> *conservatory in Kharkov. They ran up and*
> *threw their arms around me and screamed,*
> *"My God! You're alive!" I was petrified.*
> *I was trying to get away from people who*
> *knew us. There was nothing we feared*
> *more.*

These people knew the girls' real names,
they knew Zhanna and Frina were Jewish.
Zhanna knew
they had to get away from Poltava.
If one of their acquaintances slipped . . .

But it was Zhanna who slipped.

NAMING NAMES

It happened back
at Professor Oleg's house
when Frina was visiting.
Oleg heard the girls chatting
and Zhanna made a terrible mistake.
She called her sister by her real name—
Frina, not Marina.

Oleg heard and demanded to know
what was going on.
Who was Frina? Why were they lying?

Although he was Russian,
he was the Nazi commandant's right-hand man.
Would he tell?
With their aliases exposed,
there was no going back.

Zhanna fell apart.
In tears, she told Oleg everything.

COMPASSION

Oleg listened.
Although he worked for the Nazis,
he was first and foremost a Russian.
He told the girls they could not stay.
They would be discovered as Jews,
they would be killed.

Oleg advised them to go to Kremenchug,
a smaller town about 70 miles south.
Once there, he told them to knock on doors,
tell their story, and add to it.
He told them to ask for their aunt—
a nonexistent aunt.
Then he hoped
they would be directed to an orphanage.

Oleg hired some farmers
to take the girls from Poltava.
Still without papers,
they set off in the April sun,
two weeks after Zhanna's real fifteenth birthday,
on the back of a cart
with squawking chickens.

TRAVELING ON

Goodbye Cities and Towns
Oh the Roads
Oh the Roads
In the Forest, Front line
Wide is my Motherland
Oh the Roads
Oh the Roads
Sunset over Mountain
Dark Night
Oh the Roads
Oh the Roads
Forward to Meet the Sunrise
To the New Home
Oh the Roads
Oh the Roads

TELLING THEIR TALE

In Kremenchug,
the girls did as Oleg advised,
telling their tall tale to the first person
who opened the door.

> *My name is Anna Morozova. I am from*
> *Kharkov. My sister Marina and I are*
> *orphans. Our father was an officer in the*
> *Red Army and was killed in action. Our*
> *mother died in the bombing of Kharkov.*
> *We are looking for our aunt Morozova who*
> *lives here.*

The girls received
a most unexpected response.
The woman at the door
listened sternly, but then lit up!
Aunt Morozova?
Why, she was her dear friend!
(Moroz means frost in Russian,
so it was a common name.)

Manya Morozova had lived on that very street!
The woman was sorry to tell them

that their "aunt" had recently died,
but her "nieces" were most welcome.

The woman called out to her neighbors,
all friends of "Aunt Morozova,"
who crowded around the girls.
It was almost comical.
Dumbfounded, Zhanna and Frina
smiled and spluttered.

> *Before we knew it, they had started a lively*
> *remembrance session about their beloved*
> *neighbor. We hoped they would continue . . .*
> *because we knew nothing about this woman*
> *who was supposed to be our aunt.*

Zhanna and Frina tried to slip away,
saying they had to get to an orphanage,
but the neighbors wouldn't hear of it.
Two gallant young policemen
offered them a room,
and their neighbors—
an older man and his wife—
offered them the use of their piano.
With no other shelter,
the girls accepted for now,

but worried about how long
they could spin stories
about their fake "aunt,"
a woman they didn't know.
The next few days were uncomfortable,
full of risk.
They still needed papers,
so Zhanna set out to find
the orphanage.

NO OTHER PLACE

It was a long walk to the orphanage
on the other side of town,
but Zhanna had taken long walks before.
When she arrived, Zhanna strode inside
and spoke to the man in charge.

He explained that they housed
mostly very young children
and had little food—
mostly cucumbers from the garden.
The children found the rest of their food
by picking through the Germans' garbage.
But the director offered her and her sister beds.

The girls were one step closer
to getting identity papers.
Zhanna accepted, retrieved Frina,
and they moved straightaway
into their new home.

CUCUMBERS AND LICE

What the director said was true.

> *We had cucumbers, really bad, rotten*
> *cucumbers, and saw the little children cry*
> *from hunger. We would go through the*
> *German garbage and find something—a*
> *[meat bone] we would suck on. The sheets*
> *on the beds were covered with lice. Big lice.*
> *But I knew I had to stay there. There was*
> *no other place.*

The girls might have been hungry,
and disgusted by the insects
they'd have to shake from their sheets,
but otherwise, the orphanage was safe.

Best of all,
Zhanna and Frina
would finally get their papers,
proof to the world that they were indeed
Anna and Marina Morozova.

They didn't know it yet,
but there was one more obstacle
standing in their way. . . .

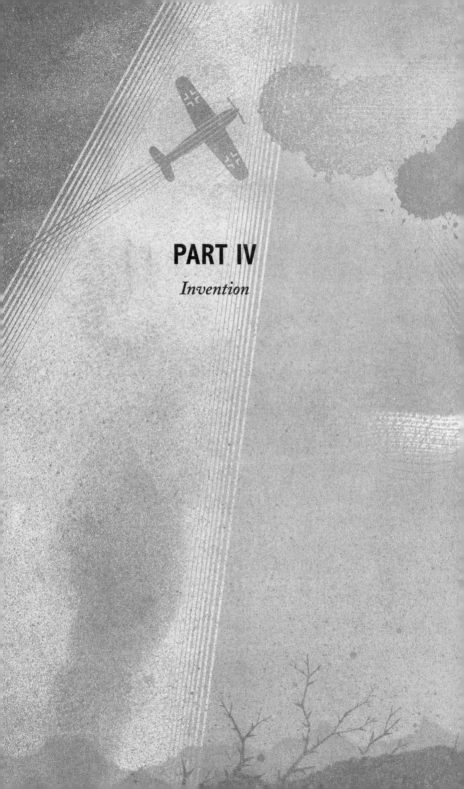

PART IV

Invention

BACK FROM THE DEAD

There was one important step
before the girls could receive
their identity papers.
Blood tests.

Zhanna heard a terrifying rumor—
that Germans could identify Jews
by their blood.
Could that be true?

Frantic, Zhanna approached
a young woman pharmacist
she had met in town.
She would have to confide in her
and reveal their true identity.

> *I counted on her humanity. She said, it's a
> lie. They can't identify any blood.*

So the girls went ahead
and made an appointment
at the documentation office,
ready to take the blood tests,
which were never actually requested.

The officials simply asked
their names and dates of birth.
The girls answered with their aliases:
Anna Morozova, born December 25, 1927;
Marina Morozova, born December 20, 1929.
The girls received green identity papers—
signed, stamped, delivered.

> *Oh, it was a big day. We were identified*
> *and we were legal.*

At long last,
Zhanna and Frina had proof
to back up their aliases,
proof they were who they said they were—
Russian girls, not Jewish.
They had solid, uncontestable proof!

It felt as big as a birthday,
as momentous as a rebirth,
as miraculous as reincarnation.
   Like coming back from the dead.

THE OLD UPRIGHT

The orphanage didn't have much,
but it did have an upright piano.
It was old and out of tune,
but oh, what a joy
to sit down and play again
after all the months of
death and desperate escapes.
The familiar melodies
washed over the girls,
restoring and refreshing them,
as a long drink of water
and a long day's sun
revive a dying plant.

That summer,
Zhanna and Frina took turns
entertaining the other children
of the orphanage,
playing sing-along songs
and practicing their Chopin.
Zhanna pulled out her precious sheet music
for Chopin's *Fantaisie-Impromptu*
that she had carried under her shirt,
close to her heart all this time.

She didn't need it to play, of course,
but here in the orphanage
at the edge of town,
far from attention,
she could relax.

She and Frina hoped
to live out the war here
where no one would know about them,
no one would bother them.

WHISPERS ON A SUMMER BREEZE

Zhanna and Frina
couldn't contain word of their talent
any more than they could stop the wind
whispering through the trees.
As they played inside the orphanage,
the lovely notes wafted out the window
and attracted passing German soldiers.

The orphanage director
felt such pride at this attention
that he offered to hire a piano tuner,
to bring the old off-key instrument
up to par with his performers.
He asked Zhanna to check the tuner's work
before he paid him.

Zhanna wanted no part of this.
She was wary of new people
coming to the orphanage,
scared to attract attention.
But how could she refuse?
If she made a big deal
of the simple request,
would it make the director wonder why?

She had no choice but to agree.

That's how Zhanna was discovered.

THE TUNE-UP

The piano tuner arrived—
a friendly, intelligent, professional man
named Misha Alexandrovich.
He sat hunched over his work,
tapping, tweaking, and tinkering.
When he was finished,
Zhanna sat down to test the piano
so he could be paid.

> *I played Beethoven or something and he*
> *said, "This is crazy. We don't have anybody*
> *that plays that well in Kremenchug. You've*
> *got to go play for the directors of the music*
> *school." And I started to shiver.*

The tuner persisted,
and Zhanna resisted,
insisted
she wanted to stay in the orphanage.
He urged her again and again
to come with him.
Again and again, she said no.

He said, "What do you mean, no? There
is nothing for you to eat here. You are
starving to death. You will be fed there."

In the end, he wore Zhanna down.
She and Frina were forced to agree;
saying no would only arouse suspicion.

THE MUSIC SCHOOL

Misha escorted Zhanna and Frina to town
and introduced them
to the director of the music school,
Professor Bulbenko.

> *She was a wonderful lady, so alive and*
> *sweet. She went wild for our playing.*
> *"You have to live here and practice!" she*
> *said. We were frightened and rightfully*
> *so. I said, "No, we have a place." We tried*
> *not to . . . tried very hard. But she adored*
> *music so much and was begging us to stay.*
> *So there was nothing to do but move into*
> *our new quarters.*

Zhanna and Frina were given a studio—
two cots in a practice room
beside a piano.
Goodbye, lice! Goodbye, cucumbers!
They had enough to eat,
new friends who adored music,
a new home.

But there was a catch.

A FAVOR?

Professor Bulbenko
soon made a request,
one that filled Zhanna with foreboding,
like the opening bars
of Beethoven's Fifth.
The professor needed pianists
to play for her singers and dancers
who were required to perform
for the Germans
at the local theater next door.
There were precious few forms
of entertainment at the time,
besides music and the theater.
The professor pleaded for their help.
Play for the Nazi officers?
It was like asking
a rabbit to jump out of a hat
for an audience of wolves.
They could eat her alive.

I have spent months running and hiding
from the Nazis, and now you are going to
put me—a fugitive Jew—on a stage before
hundreds of German soldiers?

Once again, there was no easy way to refuse.

AUDITIONING

Zhanna and Frina
had no special clothes
to wear for their theater audition.
In fact, they had no extra clothes at all.
Somewhere along the way,
their sapphire-blue concert dresses
had disappeared,
as had their papa's coat,
forgotten in their desperate flight,
left behind in the snow, on the train,
they didn't know.

Now all they had
were the dingy dresses and shabby shoes
they had worn every day since
the roundup of Jews in Kharkov.
Zhanna's shoe had a hole in it.
She couldn't hide
her big toe poking through.

She arrived at the theater
and had to wade through a gauntlet
of good-looking dancers, singers, and actors,
unimpressed with these girls,
with these so-called prodigies.

They were all well-dressed, and when
they saw my toe sticking out, they burst
into laughter. It was not funny. These
clothes were all I had. It hurt me. I
thought, "I will never forget this."

Zhanna had the last laugh.
There was no audition.
Zhanna and Frina were hired on the spot,
based on the professor's recommendation.
They were offered a generous salary,
more than anyone else snickering outside.

It would be all right.
Now the girls would have paying jobs!
Sure, there would be Nazis in the audience,
but Zhanna reassured herself that
she would play piano on the sidelines.
No one would really see her there.
They would be watching
the singers and dancers on stage.
Part of her wanted to hide in the shadows.
But part of her wanted to overshadow
those awful people who had laughed at her.
It wasn't long before she got her chance.

FLYING SOLO

The theater director
knew star power when he saw it.
He quickly realized his biggest attraction
was not his dancers, singers,
jugglers, or actors.
Not even his handsome balalaika player.
It was the young girl
with the hole in her shoe.
He proudly offered Zhanna
a solo performance,
center stage for all to see.

Professor Bulbenko was eager to help.
She made Zhanna a knee-length,
off-white silk dress,
bought her new shoes,
and helped put her hair in pigtails.

Zhanna chose a piece
she could play by heart—
the Chopin Scherzo in B-flat Minor.
She was confident about her performance,
but fearful that she might be recognized.
She had been so famous

that any one
of the 600 German, Italian,
and Austrian officers
packing the concert hall
might remember her.
They might see that Anna Morozova
was really Zhanna Arshanskaya.

> Was there time to run? No.
> Was there a place to hide? No.

She saw the other performers,
pointing and whispering,
taking their seats behind the officers.
She decided to take a stand.

> *I was still angry at [them laughing] at*
> *my shoes. When I walked out to play . . . I*
> *thought, "Let's see if you ever laugh at me*
> *again."*

Anger sparked a flame within Zhanna
that blazed sky-high as she played.
INDIGNATION at the performers who laughed at her,
FURY at the Nazis who had killed her family,
RAGE at the injustice in the world

ignited her fingers on the keyboard
and sent Chopin's notes rocketing to
the heavens and back.
With expertise and emotion,
Zhanna played her fury out,
        played her fear out
            played her heart out.

BRAVA! BRAVA!

Zhanna's acclaim spread far and wide
after that first night's standing ovation.
No one had recognized her, as she had feared,
and now she had fans with flowers,
comrades with cakes,
and suitors with schnapps,
waiting outside her door,
calling to her and Frina at their window.
      Nazi fans.
They had no idea that the two little girls,
the objects of their affection,
of their adoration,
were Jewish.

> *They would stand by the window and*
> *serenade us. They just loved the music. They*
> *were dying of boredom and . . . adored the*
> *military marches by Schubert. I played the*
> *Grieg concerto seven nights in a row.*

At the theater, the soldiers demanded
more, more, more!
Encore! Encore!

Zhanna played day and night—
four-hand pieces with Frina,
spotlighted solos,
plus accompaniments for the
dancers, singers, actors, and jugglers.

Rehearsals started early,
performances ended late,
seven days a week.
Zhanna was paid handsomely
because the acts couldn't go on without her.
Too bad there was nothing to buy.

YOU HAVE TO BE ON YOUR TOES

Working together day in and day out,
Zhanna and Frina made friends,
a close family of wonderful friends,
with the other young people in the troupe.

The handsome balalaika player named Markov
noticed Zhanna and followed her,
like a lovesick pup.
Zhanna was charmed by him,
but soon saw him for the flirt he was.

> *He was a terrific soul, but unbearable with*
> *women. He was after me all the time,*
> *grabbing at me. I found myself running*
> *from him as fast as I could.*

Some of the ballerinas weren't friendly.
They were used to being on the receiving end
of bouquets tossed onstage
and nightly cries of "Brava, Brava!"
They were used to handsome men
flocking to *their* doors.
They were *not* used
to bending over backward

for two young girls
deemed essential to rehearsals.
They were not used
to being upstaged by teenagers
who were, quite handily,
stealing the show.

> *They got furious when they found out that*
> *my salary was the highest in the theater.*
> *The director was grateful to me because*
> *I could work endlessly. I never stopped.*
> *Anything they needed me to play, I would.*

Zhanna still worried
about being recognized.

Little did she know
that some of the newer ballerinas
        had come from Kharkov.

Little did she know
that betrayal
was brewing backstage.

SPINNING SECRETS

Round and round a secret swirls! Who can vouch for these young girls? Rumor has it they are Jews. Who will tell and spread the news?

TROUBLEMAKERS

The dancers from Kharkov
set the rumors whirling.

> *They decided to go to the German bosses*
> *with the rumor that we were Jews. They*
> *were idiots to do this. Without us there was*
> *nobody to play and they would have no jobs.*

Without Zhanna and Frina,
the dances, concerts, and plays
would not go on.
The commandant's girlfriend
would be out of work.
His soldiers would have no entertainment,
no music to soothe them,
no nightly relief from their deadly days.

The commandant was inclined
to dismiss the ballerinas
but
they offered proof—
a woman sewing costumes backstage
had a son who had known Zhanna and Frina
in the Kharkov Conservatory.

The officer had no choice
but to investigate.
He called the woman and her son to his office.
If they confirmed
that Zhanna and Frina were Jewish,
the girls would be arrested.

                              Or worse.

THE MEETING

The terrified woman
and her son were summoned
and interrogated by the Nazi officer.

They resolutely faced the commandant,
mustered all their courage . . .

       and lied.

The woman said that she knew
Zhanna and Frina's parents
and they were not Jewish.
She accused the dancers of lying
because they were jealous.
That was enough proof
for the commandant.

*The woman and her son put their lives on
the line for us. But I was never at peace
after that. The rumor was still out there.
We could get caught at any moment.*

Rumors, even discredited rumors,
have a nasty way of spreading.
And the truth has a way of coming out.
Zhanna and Frina had to be extra careful now.

PUBLICITY

Of course, the theater director
wanted to showcase his talent.
Of course, he wanted to take
publicity photographs of his players.
The last thing
Zhanna and Frina wanted
was to have their photos circulated.
The sisters argued about what to do.

Frina refused to go to the shoot.
Zhanna knew that their absence
would attract attention,
too much attention.
So with great reluctance
she went to sit for the photo.

To her horror, she was
positioned in the center of the performers.
There was only one thing
she could think to do,
only one thing
that might help her hide a bit.
Snap! Click! Flash!
The final photo shows more than

thirty young people
looking straight ahead, smiling.
Only one girl in the center
is turning away,
the seriousness
of this exposure in her eyes.

COMMAND PERFORMANCES

Just as peony buds burst
into ever larger globes,
so Zhanna and Frina's world opened up.

Their concerts attracted attention,
and Nazis claimed these talented girls,
these prize flowers, for their own.

They were asked to play
at more exclusive venues.
Instead of playing in a large theater
for hundreds of German soldiers,
they were asked to perform
for small dinner groups
of German officers
in private dining rooms.
There was no saying no.
Misha, the piano tuner
from the orphanage,
who was now a good friend,
would escort them.

When Zhanna and Frina arrived
in their finest dresses,

they were quietly greeted by a handful
of impeccably groomed field generals
and other Nazi officers.
All of Zhanna's hopes
for remaining anonymous,
for remaining out of reach,
disappeared.
The Nazis had reeled her in
and now she and her sister
were on display,
the catch of the day,
just an arm's length away.
The Nazis could see them up close—
the color of their eyes,
the length of their lashes,
the curve of their wavering smiles.

But they didn't have to worry.
The officers were cordial and courtly.
It was hard to believe
that these dashing gentlemen by night,
redolent with sweet-smelling cologne,
awoke as barbarian brutes by dawn,
killing Jews like her and her sister
day in and day out.
It was hard to believe that

they transformed overnight
like werewolves
awakened not by the moon,
but by dawn's first light.

On that first night,
the Germans nodded to the girls,
gesturing an invitation
to dine with them.
Due to the language barrier,
they ate in relative silence.
After their meal,
the girls were invited to play
and they obliged,
launching into Chopin, Schubert,
Beethoven, and Brahms.
The refined officers didn't talk,
but respectfully leaned back
and truly listened.

*These were very serious people, a wonderful
audience. They kept saying, "Noch
einmal!"—once more!—over and over.*

How could she do it?
Play for the enemy

who had killed her family?
Zhanna remembered her father's words:
"I don't care what you do. Just live."
This was what it took to stay alive.
So Zhanna closed her eyes and played
for the memory of her family.

After that night, the invitations poured in,
and each time the applause was heartfelt.
Like the apothecaries
back in Berdyansk
mixing their brews,
Zhanna and Frina worked their magic.
For a few short hours,
the world's greatest composers
lifted the Jewish girls and Nazi officers
to the same lofty plane
high above the hatred and horrors of war.
The music reminded them all
what it felt like to be human again.

ON THE RUN

Zhanna dreamed of the day
the Soviets' Red Army
would return
to rescue them
from the Germans—
the day the Nazis would turn tail and run,
the day she could return
to her studies, her concerts,
playing *as herself* at home in Kharkov.
Would there ever come a day
when she wouldn't have to hide
behind her alias,
a magical day
when Anna could turn back into Zhanna?

Whenever Zhanna and Frina could steal away,
they'd scan the horizon with hopeful eyes,
watching for the Red Army's return.
They'd point out smoke in the distance
and listen for artillery fire,
but rescue did not come.

Then, in late 1942,
it seemed that Zhanna's wish

might be coming true.
The girls heard news of a great battle—
the Battle of Stalingrad
in southern Russia.
The Germans and Soviets
had attacked each other
in one of the deadliest
and bloodiest conflicts of the war.

Hitler wanted Stalingrad desperately—
for its gun industry,
for its shipping route,
and most of all
for its *name*.
If Hitler could conquer the city
named for Stalin,
what a triumph it would be!
Protecting that name
made the Soviets fight even harder
(on pain of death from their leader).

From late summer,
through the fall and early winter,
desperately brutal months,
the Soviets' Red Army fought.
"Not a step back!" decreed Stalin.

The Soviets circled the Germans,
tightening the noose,
starving them out,
and won the battle in February 1943.

As the seasons turned, so did the war.
By late summer the Nazis were on the run
fleeing back to Germany,
trying to cover their war crimes
as they went.

The Soviets chased them west,
liberating cities along the way—
Kharkov, then Kiev,
and soon, Kremenchug.
The girls would be free!

Or so they thought.

A RUDE AWAKENING

Nazi soldiers rapped on the sisters' door
and ordered them to pack.
The Germans' prize possessions—
Zhanna, Frina,
a dozen dancers and actors,
the balalaika player and juggler—
were being "evacuated" with them.
Their friend Misha
and the mother and son
who had lied for them were going too.
Zhanna's dreams of liberation dissolved,
replaced by an alarming reality.
She and her sister
were no longer revered musicians,
allowed to live relatively freely
in Kremenchug.
Now they were prisoners.

NO ESCAPE

The girls were heavily guarded.

> *I could not even go to the bathroom*
> *without guards. They would lead me there*
> *and stand outside the door, then take me*
> *back to my room.*

Escorted to a train,
the group traveled to a forest
on the Polish border.
Where were they?
Where were they headed?
The troupe's best dancer had had enough.
He tried to escape.

> *He thought he could run away and hide*
> *in the woods. They found him and put*
> *him against a wall and beat him severely*
> *in front of us. It was so horrible that I*
> *cried and could not watch. So that's how*
> *running was.*

Soon they were shepherded
onto another train,

and the group left Poland.
They said goodbye
to all they had ever known.
                    As the train rushed west,
                    Zhanna felt her true identity
                        shrinking in the distance,
                        slipping farther and farther away,
                            left behind.

Zhanna didn't know
where they were going,
but she sensed that her secret identity
was more important than ever.
                    She knew her alias Anna—
                        her mask,
                        her shield
                        her body armor—
        had to grow bigger now.

It had to cover her.
            It couldn't slip.

And she was right.
The train and its prisoners were hurtling
toward the home of Hitler's headquarters,
        barreling into the belly of the beast.

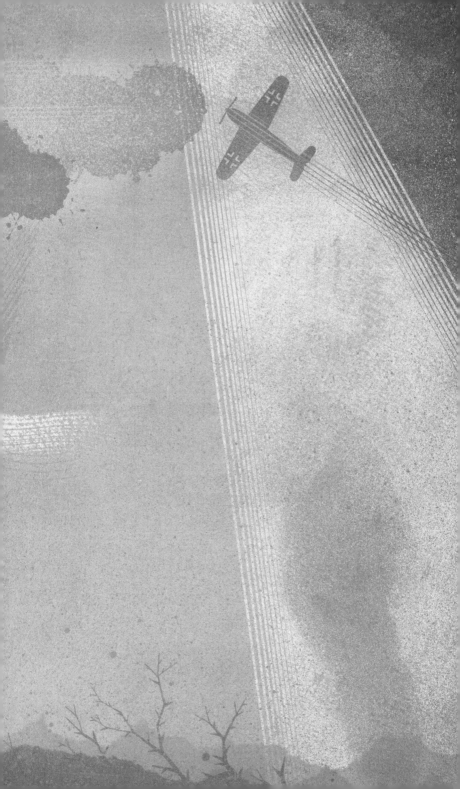

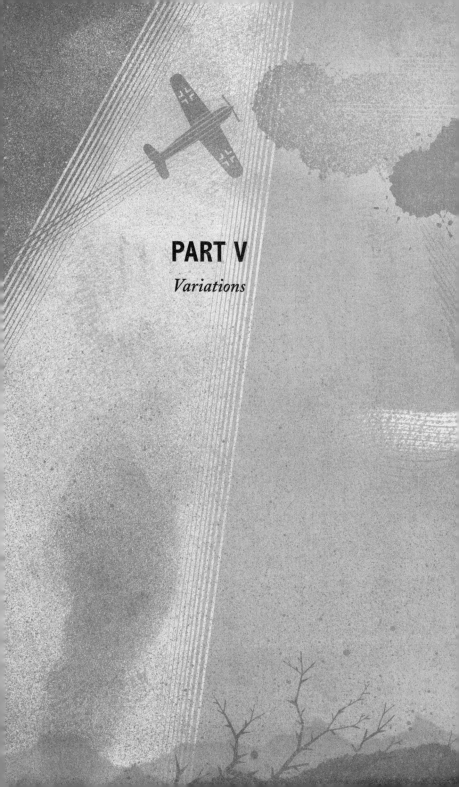

PART V

Variations

BERLIN

Biting November winds blew
as the train pulled into Hitler's capital city.
Zhanna was surprised by what she saw.

> *I was amazed. The buildings had beautiful*
> *black marble exteriors. All the windows*
> *were intact—the glass shining. The streets*
> *were extremely clean, no trash. Everything*
> *was orderly and well taken care of. I saw*
> *Berlin the way Berlin was supposed to*
> *be, as it was intended to be by the Führer*
> *for his chosen ones, so they could breathe*
> *easy and enjoy their cherished sense of*
> *superiority.*

The girls were led to their new home
in an office building
converted into a dormitory,
given food rations,
and let off the leash.
They were free to explore the city
draped with black swastikas on red flags,
a place that was crawling with Nazis,
saluting each other.

They were only a few blocks away
from Hitler himself.

> *It felt like they were next door—that Hitler*
> *might be right there. We knew we had*
> *better be good, better be lucky. If someone*
> *found out that we were Jews, we could be*
> *in the Gestapo station in two minutes.*

There they stayed, being good,
awaiting orders
about where they would be sent next.
Somebody in the group had an accordion.
To pass the time, first Zhanna
and then Frina learned to play.
They sang Russian songs
and played the squeeze-box.
Seven days later,
the Allies put the squeeze on them.

BOMBS AWAY!

A sharp rap on the door and
the $w \ldots a \ldots i \ldots l$ of the air raid siren
woke the girls and the rest of the troupe.
They were ordered to get up and *run!*
To take cover in the basement
four stories down.

The Nazis had bombed London
for 57 nights in a row in 1940.
It was called the Blitz,
short for Blitzkrieg, or lightning war.
Now, on the night of November 18, 1943,
the British Royal Air Force came for Berlin,
with more than 400 bombers
dropping their loads.
They set the city afire,
and left thousands of citizens
homeless or dead.

Zhanna and Frina
were among those fleeing disaster.

> *We ran for our lives to the nearest bunker.*
> *The bombing never ceased after that,*
> *several times a night.*

The routine was terrifying,
but sadly, nothing new
for Zhanna and Frina,
who had been bombed by the Germans
and other Axis powers in Kharkov.
Now, in Berlin,
they were helpless victims once again,
caught in the middle,
bombed by the other side, the Allies.
All Zhanna could think of was sleep.

> *It was torture going up and down the
> stairs for air raids while you were mostly
> asleep. If it were [up to] me, I would not
> have gone down. We were growing, we
> needed sleep, and we couldn't get it. We
> were worn out and miserable.*

ON THE RAILS

Before long, the sisters' troupe
was traveling again,
happy to escape
the relentless destruction in Berlin.
For the next two years,
the girls and the troupe crisscrossed
the countryside of the Third Reich by train,
stopping each day to perform.
They traveled for weeks
and sometimes months at a time,
riding the rails
south to Czechoslovakia,
back and forth,
back and forth,
often being bombed
or strafed by Allied warplanes.
When the guns from the planes rained down,
the train *SCREECHED* to a stop
and passengers fled,
taking cover under the railroad cars.
Shaken and bruised,
they would board again after a time
and continue their journey.

UNLIKELY AUDIENCES

The troupe was under orders
to perform for the poor souls
of the German slave labor camps—
the Ostarbeiter, or eastern workers.

> *We went from one slave labor camp to*
> *another. Every morning we got up early*
> *and they took us to another place. We*
> *hardly ever stayed two days in the same*
> *place. Not one minute to get comfortable—*
> *never. You play, you sleep, you go.*

Their audiences consisted of
Poles, Czechs, Russians,
Latvians, Estonians, and Ukrainians
who were forced to work
for little pay and few rations
on the farms, in the factories.
All they had in common was misery
and the OST (for Ostarbeiter) badge
they were forced to wear.

Why did the Nazis entertain
the prisoners in these camps?

Was it to help them forget
being beaten, starved, and overworked?
To discourage escapes?
For propaganda?
To show the world how well
they treated their "volunteers,"
their "guest workers"?

> *They pretended they were very*
> *humanitarian people.*

A CHANCE TO ESCAPE?

The troupe traveled with German escorts,
not guards, because escape was futile.
Zhanna's friend Markov,
the balalaika player,
tried once to escape,
but he was caught and brought back.
The troupe was traveling
in and out of war zones
and the front was dangerous.
Better to stay with the group.

ONSTAGE AT THE OSTARBEITER CAMPS

Upon arrival at an OST labor camp,
the troupe would play one-hour shows
for the people Hitler called "subhuman."
To a Nazi, only one other kind of person
was lower.
People like Zhanna and Frina.

Nothing was lower
than a Jew.

And as far as the Nazis knew,
there were no Jews in the labor camps.
Or in the troupe.
As far as the Nazis knew,
Jews were either dead in the ravines
or soon to be dead in the concentration camps.
But there were still anti-Semites in Zhanna's troupe
who would like to prove that the Nazis were mistaken.

GREEN-EYED MONSTERS

Once again, it was the ballerinas
who eyed Zhanna and her sister with envy.
Their betrayal hadn't worked before,
so they decided to try again,
going to the new officer in charge.

And once again, the mother and son
who had known the girls
in Kharkov Conservatory
were summoned
before the authorities to testify.

Once again, the mother and son were terrified.
      Once again, they lied.
            Once again, the sisters survived.

The German boss was relieved.

> *He needed us. We didn't drink, we didn't*
> *run around, and we could play. They liked*
> *the music. That's all he needed.*

FRIENDLY FIRE

The ballerinas were foiled again.
Zhanna and Frina still feared
being recognized by others.
Now that danger was compounded
in the OST camps.
The great majority of the workers
(2.2 of the 2.8 million
snatched from the streets)
came from Zhanna's homeland—Ukraine.
Many were the people who had stood by,
as they watched the Nazis round up Jews.
Their luck had run out.

Now that Zhanna and Frina
were playing in the camps,
they could encounter a friend,
a neighbor, a classmate, a fan.
It could happen
anywhere,
anytime.
    And one day it did.

A young woman from the audience
approached the girls after their performance.

She smiled and introduced herself as Lena,
happily explaining that she knew them,
she knew their cousin Tamara,
had heard them play in Tamara's apartment.

Zhanna spluttered denials—
Lena was mistaken,
they didn't have a cousin named Tamara.

But Lena knew better.
She called them by their nicknames—
Zhannachka and Frinachka.
She mentioned Professor Luntz.

It was all too much.
Lena knew the truth.
> She knew they were lying.
> She knew their real names.
>> She knew they were Jewish.

A PROMISE

Zhanna begged Lena not to tell.
She pleaded for their lives.
After all this time,
running, hiding, lying,
this couldn't be the end,
could it?
This poor young girl,
a prisoner herself,
who had nothing,
no one,
wouldn't be the one to
betray them.
          Would she?

Lena promised not to tell.
A guard led her away,
back to her life of backbreaking slave labor.

Would she think of Zhanna and Frina
in the coming days,
envious of their relative freedom?
Would she change her mind and betray them?
Or would the music and memory
of their shared childhoods

provide some small relief
from her misery?
Would Lena survive this war?

Zhanna and Frina didn't know.
They never saw her again.

D-DAY

June 6, 1944, the day known as D-Day,
a day that would live forever,
meant nothing to Zhanna and Frina.

The Nazi propaganda machine in Berlin
smothered the news.
The girls didn't know that on that day,
156,000 Allied troops
landed on a beach in France,
marking the beginning of the end
of World War II in Europe.

They didn't know that
troops from the United States,
the United Kingdom, Canada, and France
attacked the Germans that day
with almost 7,000 ships
and more than 3,000 planes.

They didn't know that rescue was on the way,
that all of northern France
would be liberated by that August,
that the Germans would be defeated
the following spring.

Help was coming.
The Allies were winning.
Zhanna and Frina had no idea
that their long ordeal would soon be over.
No one told them.
They didn't know.

GUEST APPEARANCE

The girls traveled back and forth
between the camps
and their home base in Berlin.
One day in Berlin,
there was a surprise in store for the troupe,
a special command performance—
for them.

Zhanna and Frina
didn't know what to expect.
A man entered
and took his place at the piano.
Zhanna studied his face
and realized she knew him!
It was Victor Topilin—
the pianist who had shown her
the power of the piano
at the conservatory in Kharkov
so many years ago.
She had been only eight years old
when Topilin stirred something special in Zhanna.
Now, despite his talent and passion,
he was a prisoner, just as she was.

As Topilin sat down to play,
the rich tones of Bach, Beethoven,
Chopin, and Schumann
swept over Zhanna again.
With it, her happy childhood,
and her years at the conservatory,
came rushing back and
she couldn't help it.
She started to sob.

> *All the memories—our parents, Kharkov,*
> *Berdyansk—they all came back when I*
> *heard the music. It was just too much for*
> *me. Too much beauty in hell. But suddenly,*
> *I understood why I must return to school,*
> *to a great teacher, and a musical life. I*
> *wanted to play this way, like Topilin,*
> *when the war [ended].*

DARE TO IMAGINE

When the war ended . . . ?
Would it ever happen?
And if so, where would they go?
Markov, the balalaika player,
was still smitten with Zhanna,
                even more so.
Their time together in the troupe,
day in and day out,
living the same life,
dodging the same dangers,
had intensified their friendship.
He begged Zhanna
to stay in Berlin after the war,
to marry him,
and eventually return to Russia.

> *He was a terrific soul, a wonderful*
> *person. I always trusted him. He was a*
> *full-blooded Communist and couldn't see*
> *staying in Germany. He believed I felt the*
> *same way and I would go.*

Zhanna had long dreamed of going home
to her birthland.

Would she go home with Markov
and start a family there?
What about Frina?

GROWING UP

Young Frina, now fifteen, had grown
as tall as seventeen-year-old Zhanna,
as accomplished as a musician,
and a superior singer.
Frina was no longer a shy little girl;
years of running by her older sister's side
made her more sure-footed,
able to take problems in stride.
The little girl who had loved staying home
by her mama's side
was now a strong-minded,
talented teenager,
who wasn't afraid to disagree
with her big sister.
                As Zhanna would soon see.

DESPERATE TIMES

The days passed and all that winter,
the Allies advanced,
bombing Germany to bits.
Berlin was squeezed
like a nut about to crack,
pressed by Allied forces from the west,
and by the USSR's Red Army
from the east.

> *Berlin was no place for human beings. The*
> *city around me was a heap of rubble. There*
> *was constant shooting and sounds of war. I*
> *needed to run away from the fire. But I felt*
> *I was betraying my countrymen.*

The Red Army was coming
and Zhanna desperately wanted
to welcome back her fellow Soviets,
to celebrate their victory,
to return with them to Mother Russia.

Not Frina.
She wanted to get away
from the Russians as much as the Germans.

It was rumored that
the other Allies were close,
with Americans to the south.
Frina saw them as her escort
out of the war.

> *My sister, quietly, but sternly, made up her
> mind to be a different person than I am,
> and she is. She refused to stay in Berlin to
> meet the Russians.*

Zhanna had an impossible choice.
She had to choose between
her sister, the only family she had left,
or her country, her homeland.
Would she choose Russia . . . and Markov?
Or her sister?

In the end, that decision
was swept aside.
Zhanna had to choose between
life and death.

WAR ZONE

It was death to stay in Berlin.
Food was scarce and the city
was only getting more dangerous.
Hitler's capital had been bombed relentlessly
by the Allies for two years
and now millions of shells rained down.
The city smelled of smoke and ash,
of charred wood, of pulverized buildings,
of rubble and ruins, of sky-high fires—
smells of suffocation, of death.
Indeed, more than
one quarter of a million people died
in the last three weeks of the war
as Stalin raced to take the city.

Stalin had heard rumors
of an American nuclear bomb
and was desperate to reach
the Germans' research facility
to find out what they knew
about this latest weapon.
Frantic for their top-secret research
and the German supply of uranium oxide,
Stalin demanded his army fight

like demons from hell.
His Red Army killed many
and tortured others;
their reputation for violence
preceded their arrival.

In Berlin, Germans were running scared
and taking revenge on foreigners,
especially Russians,
by snatching them off the street.

> *We lost three or four wonderful friends*
> *from the troupe. The SS took them and we*
> *never heard anything about them. One of*
> *the boys was a dancer, the most beautiful*
> *thing you have ever seen, a prince. He was*
> *gone forever.*

The girls could be next.
They had to escape.
There was only one way.

GHOSTING

The only way to survive
was to sneak out of Berlin,
to disappear in the smoke screen
of the falling bombs.
Could they manage to slip away
from their escorts and guards?
If the Germans saw them try to escape,
would they let them go?
Or kill them
    as they had the dancers?
It wasn't safe to stay,
but would it be safe to try to go?

> *[Frina] insisted on going away with the*
> *rest of the troupe south. She was very*
> *determined.*

Finally, Zhanna had her decision.

> *I made up my mind. "Well, it is my little*
> *sister. I'm not leaving her, so I'll go with her."*

They had to sneak away
while the Nazis weren't looking,

board a train, and head south.
The girls knew where the trains were,
they knew the schedules,
from their years of traveling
back and forth.
They had money.
It was time to go.

READY?

The sisters packed small suitcases
with a few clothes.
Adding her precious copy
of Chopin's *Fantaisie-Impromptu*,
Zhanna was ready.
She would leave her dreams
of returning to Russia behind.
For now.

The sisters and other members of the troupe
stole out of their dormitories,
blended into the crowds, and hurried down
the smoke-filled streets to the railroad station.
They found a train
headed south for Bavaria,
where some said
they would find the American troops.

All was chaos in Berlin,
so nobody stopped them.
The Germans were running too.

MAKING THEIR GETAWAY

The sisters boarded the train
to find no seats,
no food,
no water,
no bathrooms.

But there was a bigger problem.
Standing in the aisle,
Zhanna and Frina were squashed
amid angry German civilians
also fleeing Berlin.
The Germans heard the sisters
speaking Russian
and turned all their fear and anger on them,
cursing and spitting.

> *They were trying to hit us and pinch us*
> *and scratch us and insult us. I thought they*
> *were trying to murder us, but we were*
> *so jammed together it was impossible for*
> *them to use their arms in a harmful way.*
> *Otherwise, I think they would have choked*
> *us. It was so tight [on the trains] . . .*
> *humanity, so close. It was scary.*

Scarier still were the Allied warplanes
strafing the German train as it snaked
across the countryside.
Machine guns blasted
at the train's engine.
If they could disable the locomotive,
explode any ammunition aboard,
and leave the wreckage
blocking the track,
they could choke off
the Germans' supply route.

Each time the guns fired,
the train screeched to a halt
and Zhanna and Frina fled outside
with the other passengers
to take cover under the cars.
It wasn't the safest refuge,
but the only place to hide.
They returned inside
only when the gunfire stopped.

The 350-mile journey
to Augsburg near Munich
should have taken about six hours.

On Zhanna's train,
the hectic stop-and-start trip
took six days,
with the passengers standing
crammed together
like terrorized sheep in a pen.

Stopping at one station,
Zhanna found a bit of wall space,
leaned up against it,
and fell sound asleep.
Standing up.

Sleep was like bread and air.

SANCTUARY

After arriving in Augsburg,
Zhanna, Frina,
and their friends in the troupe
switched trains to escape
the spiteful German passengers.

Their final destination was Kempten,
one of the oldest towns in Germany,
close to the southern border with Austria.
Stepping off the train,
they found all was quiet
in this small and sleepy refuge,
a surreal oasis
far from the barrage of gunfire north.
The girls found shelter in an empty school
and collapsed.

> *For the first time in years, we had no fear.*
> *We slept twenty hours a day. . . . That's all*
> *we did—sleep and wait for the war to end.*

ODE TO VICTORY

Far north of Kempten,
the Russian Red Army's race
to Berlin was won!
Entering the city on April 23, 1945,
Stalin's soldiers took Berlin
block by block
with bombs, tanks,
cannons, and street artillery
facing snipers, machine guns,
and flamethrowers.

On April 30, Red Army soldiers
stormed the burned-out Reichstag building
and flew the red flag of the Soviets
from the crown of the statue *Germania*
on the roof.

That same day, Hitler committed suicide
with his brand-new bride Eva Braun,
rather than admit that his
"Thousand-Year Reich"
had lasted only twelve years.
Only.
Twelve long, murderous years.

The Soviets had paid dearly in those years,
losing an estimated 27 million citizens
by the end,
more than all other nations combined.

V-E DAY

A week later, it was over.
Germany surrendered unconditionally
on May 7, 1945,
signing official papers the following day.
May 8 became known as V-E Day
or Victory in Europe Day.
Around the world, bold headlines
shouted the long-awaited news:
"Nazis Quit"
    "Surrender Is Unconditional"
            "V-E Day—It's All Over"

Church bells pealed ecstatic relief.
After years of blackouts, rations, and bombs,
jubilation hit the streets festooned with flags,
while bonfires and fireworks lit up the night.
Millions of people turned out—
jumping in fountains, kissing strangers,
dancing and belting out songs to the tunes
of gramophones, accordions, and barrel organs.

Even the sleepy town of Kempten
couldn't suppress the news
that the war was over.

Zhanna and Frina were eager
to celebrate V-E Day.
They pulled on their very best clothes—
matching silk skirts and shirts—
and went looking for the Americans
to toast their freedom
with the liberating army.

> *We never saw a soul. We [wanted] to tell*
> *them right away who we were, our names,*
> *you know. We walked and walked and*
> *never saw them.*

All was quiet
up and down the streets
as the townspeople hid inside,
waiting to see what would happen next.

Britain's Winston Churchill
warned the world
that the war still raged
in the Pacific.
Indeed, the Japanese
wouldn't surrender
until August 14.
But for Zhanna and Frina,

their years of running and hiding
from the Nazis were

f
    i
        n
           a
              l
               l
                  y
                     OVER.

Against all odds,
these two young girls had survived.
They had done what their papa had asked.
    "Just live."

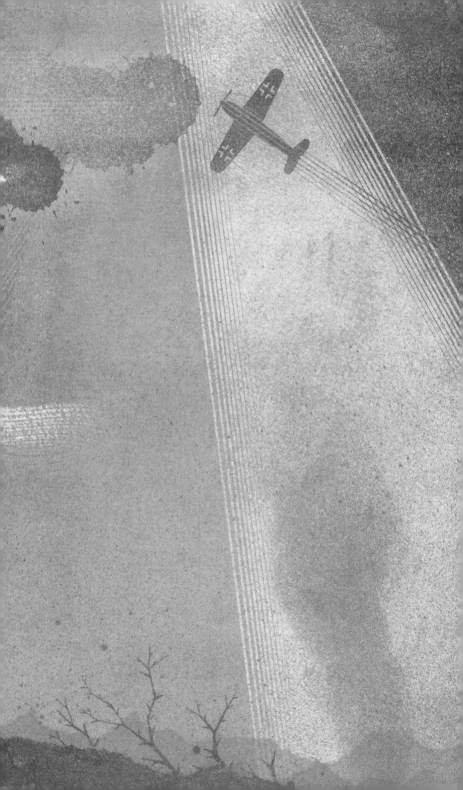

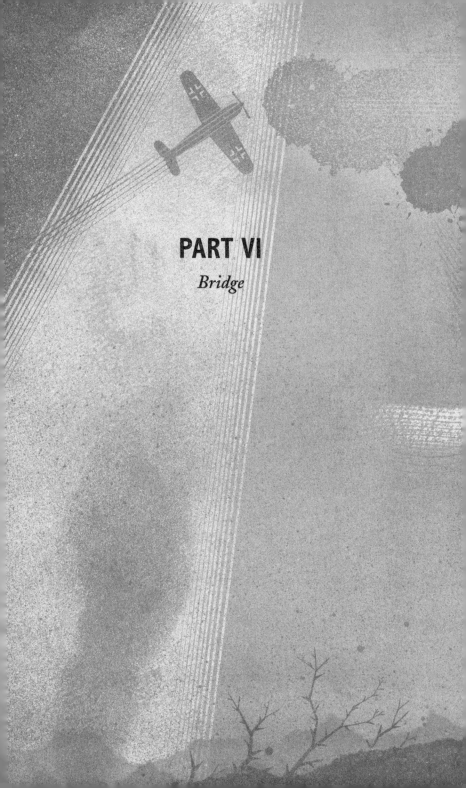

PART VI

Bridge

MISSING PIECES

The war was over,
but Zhanna and Frina found themselves
teenagers alone in a foreign land,
with no family to return to.
They had to pick up the pieces of their lives
and puzzle out what was next.
Where would they go?
Where was home?
Where would they fit in?

THE MAN WITH HIS FEET ON THE DESK

The United Nations
had set up camps
for "displaced persons"
to help answer these questions.
They helped people
like Zhanna and Frina
left strewn on the shores of war—
former prisoners,
the wounded, refugees—
until they could find a new home.
Zhanna finally found the Americans
when she went to apply
for a place at a camp one week later.

She entered the office,
not knowing what to expect.
The first surprise?
Zhanna found the man in charge
with his feet up on the desk!

> *You eat on the table and you work on the*
> *table. You don't put your feet on the table.*
> *Unheard of.*

The second surprise
was hearing English
for the first time.

> *I thought, "They must be kidding—this*
> *cannot be a language!" It was so awful*
> *that I thought they were putting on a show*
> *to amuse me.*

It was a strange new world.
Through translators and sign language,
the man arranged for the girls
to move once again
to a displaced persons camp
called Funk Kaserne near Munich,
until they could find a new home.

FUNK KASERNE

Next stop? An abandoned army barracks
housing 5,000 homeless refugees,
including Zhanna, Frina,
and the remaining members of their troupe.

Zhanna thought once again
of returning to Russia.
She filled out the appropriate paperwork
and packed her few belongings,
including her Chopin sheet music.
The camp arranged for Zhanna and Frina
to be picked up by Russian Army officers.
At the last moment, Zhanna was in for a shock.

Frina said no. She refused to go.

A SISTER'S NIGHTMARE

Just as Frina had lain down in the snow
and refused to get up,
just as she had stood up to Zhanna in Berlin,
Frina dug in her heels.
She adamantly refused to return to Russia.
For her, the Soviet Union
was a land of nightmares—
scarlet fever, starvation, Stalin's secret police,
her unspoken memory of Drobitsky Yar.

> *Frina didn't have a chance of life in*
> *Russia. She was afraid of it. She was the*
> *baby in the family until the war began.*
> *It was all too much sorrow for Frina. She*
> *wanted something different.*

Zhanna couldn't believe this was happening.
Not now. Not after all this time.

> *I thought Frina would give in, but she*
> *didn't move. It was plain that she meant it.*

Zhanna wept on her bed
as Frina watched in stony silence.

Little did Zhanna know at the time
what would come to pass.
More than five million Soviets
returned home,
some voluntarily at first,
later rounded up by Soviet forces.
Many of those who returned to Russia
with the Red Army,
as Zhanna had wanted to,
were imprisoned by Stalin for treason,
for "collaborating" with the enemy.
OST workers, prisoners of war,
refugees, and displaced persons
found in Germany?
All traitors, according to Stalin.
Expecting a "Welcome home!"
from Mother Russia,
many received a one-way ticket
to the Soviet gulags instead,
where they lived out their lives
performing backbreaking slave labor.
Or worse.

It wasn't until later
that Zhanna found out the truth.

People who returned were tortured, exiled.
Many were executed.

> *You can imagine what they did to*
> *[Markov]. They killed all the people who*
> *were in Germany. All the OST workers*
> *who were taken by force, and a person like*
> *me who was waiting for the Russians, they*
> *thought we were enemies, traitors.*

At the time,
as Zhanna was mulling over her decision
at the displaced persons camp,
she was sure of only one thing:
she couldn't leave her sister.

> *The decision was made for me.*
> *Leaving Frina was not a possibility.*

Zhanna reluctantly delivered the news
to the Red Army guards
who had come to pick them up.
They left in a huff.

Zhanna was heartbroken at the time,
thinking she would never see Russia again.

Little did she know that Frina's stubbornness probably saved her life.

AT LOOSE ENDS

Now that they wouldn't be returning to Russia,
there was nothing to do but wait.
Wait to see where else they could live.

Food at the camp consisted of
rutabaga soup, white bread,
Spam, a few crackers,

> *ugly cheese,*
> *and water with something swimming in it.*

It was enough to make
anyone want to run away.

> *It was unbelievably boring, so naturally I*
> *started walking. I walked and walked and*
> *[found] a hall with seats and a little stage*
> *with a piano. I sat down and tried it. It*
> *was an awful instrument, just horrible,*
> *but it played. I ran back to the barracks and*
> *announced, "There's a piano!" That's all it*
> *took. We decided we must put on a show.*

SHOWTIME!

The other refugees were
just as bored and restless as Zhanna.
They packed the small hall
to drink in her *Fantaisie-Impromptu*,
to marvel at the feats of the juggler,
and to join in a sing-along
of Russian folk songs.

One fan stood out from the others—
a handsome thirty-five-year-old American
in uniform,
who strode up to the girls
at the end of the show
and tried to talk to them in broken German.

> *He was so excited. He wanted to know*
> *who we were and what else we could play.*
> *He was out of his mind with curiosity*
> *about us. I thought he was one funny duck.*
> *I kept asking myself, "Does he put his feet*
> *on the table too?"*

Asking around, the girls discovered
that this "funny duck"

was the head of the camp—
Larry Dawson.
A man with big plans for the two sisters.
A man who would change their lives.

BIG PLANS

It didn't take long
for Zhanna and Frina
to see that Larry
was a dreamer, an idealist,
a man who wanted to set the world right.
He had enlisted to fight,
but his army orders assigned him
to organizing supplies for the troops
in Florida.
Not the glory of battle
he had envisioned!
At the war's end,
he heard the army's call for volunteers
to help the homeless refugees
in Europe, and he was off.
Leaving his wife, their small children,
and their farm,
he found his calling working with
the United Nations Relief
and Rehabilitation Administration
to help people like Zhanna and Frina.

A music lover himself,
he saw immediately

that the sisters needed to get back
to their music studies
derailed by the war.
They needed to focus
on technique, tone, and timing,
to practice,
to reach the peak of their potential.
Now that they weren't running for their lives,
they could turn their attention
to their first love—music.
Like someone blowing on glowing embers,
Larry would provide the spark
to feed the fire in their fingers.

He arranged special housing and practice space
with a rented piano within the camp.
Larry couldn't read music himself,
but he knew perfect pitch and tone
when he heard it.

> *I knew very well that [Larry] was a
> complete amateur, who never stopped
> talking about his brother David, the
> professional musician. But Larry had
> strong ideas about music, about the pieces
> he had heard hundreds of times, because*

that's what his family did for fun—listen
to music at home.

The girls were amused that this amateur
thought he could teach them piano,
but his kindness and passion for their music
fueled their friendship.

They still hadn't revealed their true identities
to him. Or anyone.
Larry knew them as Anna and Marina.
     But that was about to change.

TRUST AND THE TRUTH

It was one day when Larry came to visit.
He wanted to check on their progress
and see that they were getting
all the support they needed.
Chatting with his young friends, he asked,
"If you could have anything you desired
at this moment, what would it be?"

Zhanna knew immediately.
So did Frina.

Of course, they wanted their family back,
but Larry wasn't a magician.
What did they want?
It wasn't riches,
a palace,
a new wardrobe,
not even a new piano.
It was nothing that money could buy.
Zhanna looked at this kind man,
someone she knew they could trust, and said,

Our names—we want our true names back.

What?

Larry didn't understand,
so the whole story came pouring out:
how their papers were false,
how their names were aliases,
how their story was a lie,
how Anna and Marina Morozova
were really Zhanna and Frina Arshanskaya,
how they were Jewish,
            how their family had been murdered.
Zhanna began to sob.

Kneeling in front of them,
Larry made a vow right then—
that no one would ever harm them again.
He would see to it.
"You're part of my family now," he said.

For the girls, relief welled up inside them
and coursed down their cheeks,
washing away the years of worry,
washing away their masks.

> *Getting our names back, telling Larry the*
> *truth—it was like the feeling on the day*
> *the war ended. A feeling that big—to be*
> *the person you really are.*

Frina could forget the name Marina.

And Zhanna would be alias Anna no more.

CELEBRATION

It was Larry's idea to celebrate
and reintroduce
the young Jewish girls to the world
with a very special concert.
Fittingly, they would play for Polish Jews
liberated from the first
and one of the worst
concentration camps of the war—
Dachau.
There, 41,000 men, women,
and children had died,
plus thousands more
that were undocumented.
Liberated by the Allies on April 29, 1945,
there were about 30,000 survivors
found in Dachau;
a third of them barely alive.

*Larry was proud to announce that these
two Jewish girls were going to play
for the freed Jews. It would be a great
celebration—the rejoicing of people who
lived through hell together.*

Nothing but the best would do.
And they wouldn't be performing
their usual repertoire.
Larry spirited the girls away
to a luxurious home
in the Bavarian Alps.
They had two months to practice 13 pieces
he had chosen,
including new and complex compositions.

> *I had to learn [Beethoven's]* Appassionata
> *because he always loved it. And a devilishly
> difficult scherzo by Mendelssohn. Frina
> had to learn [Beethoven's] D–Minor
> Sonata, Opus 31.*

And they had to learn them on their own.
As the night of the concert approached,
Zhanna knew she wasn't ready.

> *I needed help from an experienced pianist
> and teacher. All I got from my coach was a
> lot of inspiration and unrealistic ideas.*

Zhanna and Frina would have to figure out
their new pieces for themselves.

FANTAISIE-IMPROMPTU

The night of the concert arrived.
Twelve hundred liberated Jews,
still bone-thin, sickly, and haunted
by the inhumanity
of the Dachau death camp,
took their seats before the makeshift stage.
They gazed up
at these two young Jewish girls
who, like them,
had survived against all odds.

Zhanna and Frina took their places
and in turn began to play
Beethoven, Liszt, and Chopin—
melodies from the past,
from their childhoods,
including Zhanna's cherished
Fantaisie-Impromptu—
the music she had held close to her heart
all the days of their flight.

Chopin's piece swept over everyone,
audience and artists alike that night,
speaking of the harmony and hurt
the world can hold for us all.

It sang of our improvised lives—
lighthearted burbling times,
different rhythms for different hands,
moving faster and faster into stormy sections
with octaves digging lower and lower,
becoming increasingly bleak,
then tumbling into another world—
a lull of tranquility—
only to return to storms,
to agitation,
then ah! A reprieve of quiet.
Of peace.

As she played,
Zhanna glanced out at the rapt audience
and connected to her fellow survivors.

> *I was playing, wholly tied to the listeners'*
> *hearts. I was there with them alive, with*
> *my sister, their ears connected to mine,*
> *able to hear [the music] speak. The horror*
> *created by Hitler was defeated. . . . The*
> *performance wasn't up to my standard,*
> *[but] it had done what we wanted—to*
> *lift humanity to goodness again, to fill the*
> *survivors of torture with signs of life and*
> *peace without fear.*

RHAPSODY

For the grand finale that night
the girls played their four-handed piece—
Liszt's Hungarian Rhapsody No. 2.
The sisters took their places
together on the bench,
side by side as they had been
throughout their long ordeal.

In the end, they stood together,
taking their bow together—
as the sisters, allies, co-conspirators,
and partners they were.

The crowd rose from their seats,
clapping and cheering,
stamping their feet,
triumphantly affirming the girls
as wunderkinds, as Jews, and as fellow survivors,
foretelling who they would be as women,
as master musicians,

shouting their names—

their birth names,

their Jewish names—

Zhanna! Frina!

to the heavens.

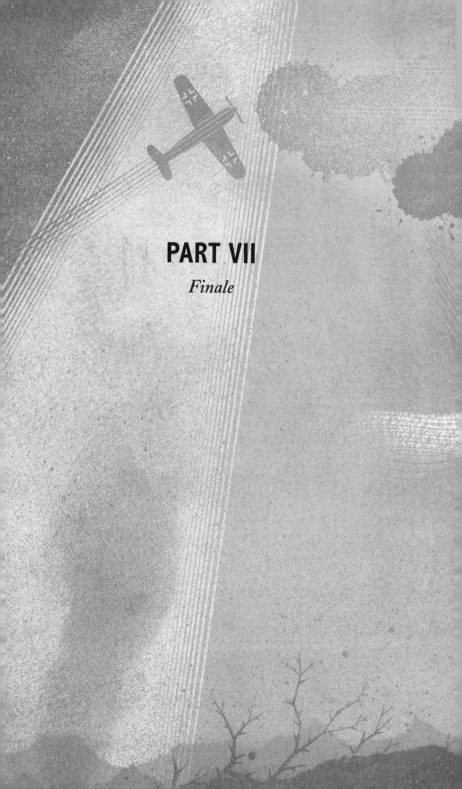

PART VII

Finale

WHAT'S IN A NAME?

Everyone thought that
Zhanna and Frina Arshanskaya had died.
In 2005, their names were etched
in the cold marble
of the candlelit underground "Room of Tragedy"
at the Drobitsky Yar memorial.

The world assumed
these two little girls had died
beside their parents and grandparents,
along with at least 16,000 Jews murdered
in the Ukrainian ravine.

In fact, Zhanna and Frina
are among the only known survivors.
Their papa had whispered,
          "I don't care what you do. Just live."

And live they did—
long and music-filled lives,
traveling to America,
making a new home
with Larry Dawson and his wife,
and auditioning for

the Juilliard School in New York City,
one of the finest music schools in the country
(indeed, the world)!
They were awarded full scholarships
to study under the masters of music
in a New World.

It was in America
that Zhanna and Frina
made names for themselves
as renowned concert pianists.

It was in America
where the girls married two musicians,
had children,
and grandchildren.

And it was in America
that a granddaughter
changed Zhanna's life.

THE LETTER

When young Aimée wrote
and asked about Zhanna's childhood
for a school history project,
her grandma wondered how to answer.

Ultimately, she decided—
with nothing but the truth.
She sent Aimée
a short and shocking letter
that revealed secrets Zhanna had kept
for fifty years.

She spoke of her childhood,
how she and her sister had lost everything—
their country, their home, their parents,
even their names.

Zhanna confided in
her thirteen-year-old granddaughter.

> *I found out how little death mattered to me*
> *if you weren't ridiculed, laughed at, or had*
> *your picture taken at your most humiliated*
> *moment. Humiliation is much worse than*
> *death. I guess our honor is life itself.*

After writing that letter,
Zhanna realized
her life story was important.
People needed to know.

THE WHOLE STORY

Zhanna finally opened up to her son,
journalist and author Greg Dawson.
He listened and researched,
traveled to Ukraine—
    visited Zhanna's house,
    the Kharkov Conservatory,
    the killing fields—
and wrote about it.
Thanks to Greg,
the happy news
of the girls' survival spread.

It spun across the world
to Zhanna's long-lost friend Svetlana,
living in Ukraine,
who *still* had the silky blue sash
that Zhanna had dropped in the snow
so long ago.

Svetlana had kept it safe
for Zhanna as she had promised she would.
One yard of silk
still tied two childhood friends
across the world,

across nearly eighty years.
In 2019, Svetlana returned it.

Now that silken keepsake
is a precious piece of history,
an heirloom that binds
Zhanna's family, friends,
and future generations,
both hers and ours,
to her story,
to her past.

REPRISE

Zhanna had bottled up
the sad story of her childhood.
She had put it away for decades,
like a dusty apothecary jar
shelved in a back room
of old Berdyansk,
until one day,
a beloved young girl lifted the lid.

Warmed by air, light, and affection,
the story bubbled up and spilled out.

It was Zhanna's story of loss and pain
that now became
      a song,
      a sonata
      dedicated to
      strength,
      sisters,
      and the music that saved them.

And it was all thanks to eighth grader Aimée
      who wrote a letter to her grandma Z.

NOTES
WHAT WE DIDN'T KNOW

Most of us have heard about the gas chambers at concentration camps like Auschwitz, Treblinka, and others, but not about the killing fields that preceded them. Most people have no idea that the Nazis' systematic mass extermination of six million European Jews began months before the permanent gassing facilities in the death camps became fully operational. In Ukraine, thousands upon thousands of Jews were murdered en masse (at Kamianets-Podolskii in August 1941, at Babi Yar that September, and in Odessa in October). Most were shot in the back and pushed into ravines. These massacres and others happened well before the December Chelmno gas van murders in Poland, and it was just the beginning. Historian Alexander Kruglov estimates that more than 500,000 Ukrainian Jews died in the second half of 1941. By 1944, almost 1.5 million Jews in the Soviet Union and eastern Europe had been assassinated in this "Holocaust by bullets." These crime scenes were quickly covered up, first by the Nazis and then by Stalin.

For the Nazis, these brutal, cold-blooded shootings took a toll on the soldiers' psyches. Some questioned killing women and children. SS chief Heinrich Himmler had a ready answer: if they didn't kill the families, the children might grow up to avenge their fathers' deaths, causing harm to German sons and grandsons.

So the gas chambers were invented to be more "humane" for the Nazis, allowing them to try to emotionally distance themselves from the killings. This method was deemed efficient, and was relatively secret, close to the Jewish ghettos, and far from prying eyes.

By the time the first concentration camps gassed their victims, most of the Jewish people in Ukraine had already been eliminated by bullets. In 1943, Soviet-Jewish journalist Vassily Grossman wrote, "In Ukraine there are no Jews. Nowhere—Poltava, Kharkov, Kremenchug, Bristol, Yagotin . . . A people has been murdered." Zhanna and her sister Frina are among the few known survivors of the estimated 16,000 men, women, and children murdered in the killing field of Drobitsky Yar.

The stories of the ravines, of Babi Yar, Drobitsky Yar, and others, continued to be covered up for decades. After the war, Stalin slammed the Iron Curtain down on the story, keeping it from the West and suppressing the truth from his own countrymen.

Novelists and poets picked up the cause, perhaps most famously Russian poet Yevgeny Yevtushenko, who wrote "Babi Yar" in 1961 and "The Apple Trees of Drobitsky" in 1989. His poems protested the Soviet Union's refusal to acknowledge the killing fields and the anti-Semitism that still pervaded his country. One section of "Babi Yar" reads:

> *The wild grasses rustle over Babi Yar.*
> *The trees look ominous,*
> > *like judges.*
> *Here all things scream silently,*
> > *and, baring my head,*
> *slowly I feel myself*
> > *turning grey.*
> *And I myself*
> > *am one massive, soundless scream*
> *above the thousand thousand buried here.*
> *I am*
> > *each old man*
> > > *here shot dead.*
> *I am*
> > *every child*
> > > *here shot dead.*
> > *Nothing in me*
> > > *shall ever forget!*

Soviet composer Dmitri Shostakovich set "Babi Yar" to music, and it became his Symphony No. 13. It was this poet, this composer, and other authors who exposed this tragedy for the world to see. Such is the power of the arts.

Even so, a memorial to those who died at Babi Yar erected in the 1970s did not identify the victims as Jewish, but simply referred to "peaceful Soviet citizens." It was only when the Soviet Union collapsed in 1991 that this tragedy was fully revealed as the ruthless extermination of Jewish people. And it wasn't until 1991, half a century after Zhanna and Frina's family and so many others were murdered, that a memorial at Drobitsky Yar was begun. The memorial opened in 2002.

The story of Zhanna and Frina is a true story. And one we should never forget.

Permission to reprint an excerpt from "Babi Yar" granted by Maria Yevtushenko

PHOTOGRAPHS

Courtesy of the Dawson Family (unless otherwise noted)

How did photos of Zhanna and Frina as children survive when the Nazis forced the family to leave Kharkov without most of their belongings? It was thanks to Zhanna's aunt and uncle, who took family photos with them when they fled east.

Zhanna at the piano, age five

Zhanna and Frina were ages eight and six when they moved to Kharkov and became the youngest students ever awarded scholarships at the famed Kharkov Conservatory of Music.

Zhanna and Frina's father, Dmitri

Their mother, Sara

Front row, left to right: Cousin Tamara, Uncle Simyon, Uncle Moisey, Frina, Mother Sara
Back row: Cousin Celia, Aunt Eve, Zhanna, Father Dmitri

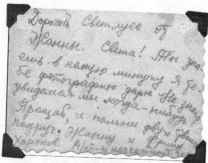

*Photo of Frina, age twelve (left),
and Zhanna, age fourteen (right),
which the girls gave to Zhanna's friend
Svetlana the day before they were marched
out of Kharkov*

To Dear Svetulya from Zhanna!
Sveta,
*You know at what kind of moment
I'm giving you this picture. I don't
know if we will ever see each other
again. Take care. Remember your two
dear friends Zhanna and Frina.*
Kharkov, 14.XII.41
sad/sorrowful year

Zhanna (left) and Frina

*The Bogancha family, who sheltered
Zhanna and Frina for two weeks
when they first escaped from the death
march. From left to right: Prokofiev
Philipovich Bogancha, Evdokiya
Nicolaevna Bogancha, and Zhanna's
classmate Nicolai Bogancha. Yad
Vashem has honored them as Righteous
Among the Nations.*

*The troupe: Zhanna, trying to hide center stage
(third row, center, with her head turned)
Frina refused to pose for this photo.*

*Lieutenant Larry Dawson
from Charlottesville, Virginia,
was head of the Funk Kaserne
displaced persons camp in
Munich, Germany.*

Larry Dawson's best friend, Ed Savage, escorted Zhanna and Frina to the SS Marine Flasher, *the ship that set sail to America on May 11, 1946.*

1947 N.Y.

Zhanna and her husband, David Dawson (brother of Larry Dawson), 1947

Frina in her early twenties

*Zhanna in her early thirties,
circa 1961*

*Zhanna with grandchildren
Chris and Aimée, 1987*

*Aimée at her high school graduation
with her grandma Z, 1999*

*Greg Dawson and Zhanna on her
eighthieth birthday, 2007*

*Zhanna with Dick Schnelker, her partner of 35 years,
circa 2008*

*Zhanna (age 93) with her daughter-in-law
Candy Dawson, 2020*

THE LETTERS

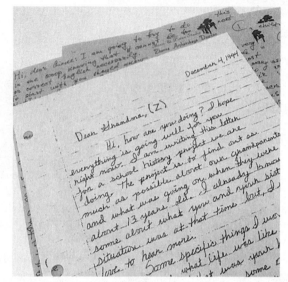

*The letter that eighth grader Aimée wrote to her grandma Z,
and Zhanna's letter in response*

HOW DID AIMÉE FEEL
WHEN ZHANNA ANSWERED HER LETTER?

"More than anything, receiving her letter felt like an act
of cosmic defiance," said Aimée. "Z doesn't like others to
tell her what to do or tell her who she is. So when the

world was convinced she *wouldn't* share, she did. It may have been a reward for my own defiant act—asking! As others said it was fruitless to ask, I did it anyway. And she responded with a gift. It felt a little like a playful dance of defiance.

"I was in middle school when I got that letter, and we all know what happens in middle school—we feel an outsized influence from others' opinions and words can cut deep. This piece at the very end of [my grandmother's] letter really hit home. Zhanna wrote, 'I found out how little death mattered to me if you weren't ridiculed, laughed at.'"

> *Humiliation is much worse than death. . . . Our honor is life itself.*　　　　　—*Zhanna Arshankaya*

Thinking of typical humiliations kids face in middle school, Aimée said, "While there were vast differences in gravity, I realized it was basically the same thing—being harassed and being humiliated and treating people poorly for things they couldn't control could, in its worst state, bubble up into [what] Hitler created—a mindset that is true bullying."

Zhanna's letter heightened Aimée's awareness of injustice, fueled even earlier by the schoolyard bullying of her brother with intellectual disabilities. She said that what she learned from Z "has been an undercurrent in all the work

I've done since then." Her volunteer work for organizations that fight bias, bigotry, and racism began shortly after learning her grandmother's story, and her advocacy for all people disadvantaged by the system continues today.

FINDING ZHANNA'S STORY
AFTERWORD BY ZHANNA'S SON GREG DAWSON

I never had the experience of being a grandson. I never rode on my granddad's shoulders or went downtown with him on Saturdays for ice cream. I never sat on my grandmother's lap as she read me *Tom Sawyer* or helped me learn how to swim. I never heard stories about where my grandparents grew up, what life was like when they were my age, and what my mom and dad were like when they were kids.

All this seemed normal to me. I never even thought about it, never asked my parents why I didn't have grandparents like other kids. The space filled by grandparents in most families was empty in mine—a vast desert devoid of family trees, stories, faces. It stretched to the horizon beyond my ken.

"Why didn't you ever ask about your grandparents?" I was sixty years old when first asked this question. It came from someone in the audience at a Barnes & Noble, where

I was speaking about *Hiding in the Spotlight*, the adult book I wrote about my mother's escape from the Holocaust. I had no answer for the baffled questioner and jokingly said I was a clueless kid only interested in sports and TV cowboys.

But I wondered, too, and the question kept coming up. The grandparents in question were my mother's parents, Dmitri and Sara, murdered by Nazis in Ukraine. Why didn't I ever ask her about them when I was growing up? To begin with, I never heard their names until I was nearly thirty years old. That's when my mother—for the first time—told me the story of how she and her sister Frina survived the Holocaust.

Still, why hadn't simple curiosity ever led me to ask Mom about her parents—*my* grandparents? Wasn't it natural to want to know? My guess is I didn't ask because my other grandparents, too, were absent from my life. My paternal grandfather died when my dad was thirteen. I have only a dim memory—a wraithlike silhouette across a darkened room—of the one time I visited my grandmother. You can't miss something that was never there.

There was something else that was never there, conspicuously missing from the home of a Holocaust survivor: Any rituals or traditions or celebrations common in Jewish homes. No synagogue, no Seder, no bar mitzvah for me or my brother. And, of course, no stories of those who perished in the Shoah. In December, we celebrated the holidays with a Christmas tree, as my dad's family had.

Ours was a thoroughly secular home—as was my mother's in Ukraine—and yet it was culturally Jewish. How could this be? Maybe the best way to explain it is to recall something my mother once said about my father, who grew up Roman Catholic in Charlottesville, Virginia: "He was the best Jew I ever knew."

A violin prodigy, my dad at age fourteen was given a scholarship to the Juilliard School of Music in New York. In those days the great majority of Juilliard students were Jewish. He absorbed and fell in love with the Jewish cultural milieu, and on weekends was invited to the homes of classmates whose mothers fed the kid from Virginia potato latkes and matzo ball soup.

It wasn't just the food that made my father the best Jew my mother ever knew. It was the shared humor and politics and music. After Juilliard, he commenced a career in which, again, he was surrounded mostly by Jews in symphony orchestras and string quartets, in the company of luminaries such as George Gershwin and Leonard Bernstein. This was the world I grew up in. When my parents threw a party most of the guests were Jewish faculty at the Indiana University School of Music. As a kid, I took it all in.

Unlike me, my children, Chris and his younger

sister, Aimée, were blessed by rich relationships with grandparents: my wife Candy's mother and father and his second wife, and my mother, Zhanna. They never knew my dad, who died four months after Chris's birth—a priceless connection short-circuited. If not for my mother's vivid presence in Aimée's life, her remarkable story would have gone untold, buried like her parents in the annals of Holocaust horrors.

Aimée was thirteen when her middle school history teacher asked students to interview a grandparent about what their life was like at the same age. Aimée, unschooled in the Holocaust and not aware of her grandmother's story, turned to "Z," as she affectionately called her. We silently wished Aimée luck in penetrating a fortress of silence, which I had breached only once, sixteen years earlier.

I had been working as a columnist at my hometown newspaper in Bloomington, Indiana, when NBC aired the groundbreaking miniseries *Holocaust*—nine and a half hours spread over four nights in April 1978. All I knew then was that my mother was a Russian refugee who came to America after the war. I hoped she had a few wartime memories I could cobble together for a column to run during the miniseries.

Gingerly, I asked her to share her memories. Grudgingly, she divulged the story she had kept from me as a child because she deemed it "too cruel" to subject young children to such things. The column ran, but my mother did not watch *Holocaust* and made it clear she had no interest in ever speaking again about her experience. So when Aimée wrote to Z with her request, we crossed our fingers and did not hold our breath.

We had underestimated the mystic bond between grandchild and grandparent. Aimée's "Dear Z" letter elicited a "Dearest Aimée" reply—four handwritten pages on eight-by-ten inch stationery—my mother relating her Holocaust experience in deeper and more personal detail than she had years earlier for my column. It rang with love for her homeland, sorrow for her lost family, fury for the Nazis—"I can never tell anyone what hatred I had for them"—concluding with a commitment to making her story "known to this world." It was a long-delayed catharsis, an unlocking of memories, a second liberation—and her granddaughter had supplied the key.

Fired by a new mission, my mother agreed to be interviewed for Steven Spielberg's Shoah Project—a video archive of survivor testimonies—and sat down with me over several years of interviews leading to the publication of two adult books about her experience and the Holocaust in Ukraine, *Hiding in the Spotlight* (2009) and *Judgment Before Nuremberg* (2012). Books with artful covers, numbered pages, and compressed narratives may give the false impression of history as an orderly beast.

Like history and life itself, book research is disorderly—a long and crooked road with hard obstacles and sweet serendipity, dry wells and gold mines, despair and triumph. The Nazis blew up Ukraine, scattering ashes to the winds. Imagine a crime scene with evidence, victims, and missing persons strewn across thousands of miles from America to Ukraine and Israel.

I thought I could write *Hiding in the Spotlight* using the interviews with my mother plus material gleaned from the internet, like the ship manifest from the SS *Marine Flasher* that brought them to America. I thought I didn't need to visit the distant crime scene. I was wrong. My first draft of *Hiding*, which I hoped was the final one, recounted the amazing facts of my mother's journey, but it didn't *feel* amazing. It lacked passion, a sense of place. "You need to go to Ukraine," Candy said.

She was right. I had to walk the streets of Berdyansk where little Zhanna roamed the bazaars, played by the sea, and joined funeral processions, bewitched by the mournful music. I had to visit the grand music conservatory in Kharkov where she and her sister Frina studied, and stand at the door of the apartment where Nazis terrorized her family. I had to see the barren field where the Arshanskys were among sixteen thousand Jews kept for two weeks in a factory with no heat or water in the dead of winter. I had to walk their final walk—their exact route, on the same day, in the same weather—to the killing field of Drobitsky

Yar. I needed to see the spot where my mother jumped out of line into the woods, cheating Hitler.

A sign under Drobitsky Yar's broken and twisted menorah memorial says, "Here the dead teach the living" in Latin, Ukrainian, and Hebrew. Photo credit: Patrick Breslin, patrickbreslin.net

Another part of the memorial complex. Photo credit: Patrick Breslin

Under the dome appears an open book engraved with one of the Ten Commandments, "Thou shalt not kill," written in ten languages. Photo credit: Tanya Zaharchenko

In 2006, Candy and I visited Ukraine and Israel. Written after our return, my second draft was twice as long and far better than the first. Only because we showed up in Kharkov was I able to visit the memorial at Drobitsky Yar and see my mother and sister Frina mistakenly listed among those murdered there. Brushing my fingers across her name etched in Cyrillic on the marble wall was surreal and chilling, like reading my own epitaph had the Nazis not let this one girl get away.

Beneath the white dome is the candlelit "Room of Tragedy," where 4,300 known names of the more than 16,000 victims are etched into the walls. Greg Dawson, Zhanna's son, points to Zhanna's and Frina's names, which were mistakenly included. In fact, the sisters are among the only known survivors. Photo credit: Candy Dawson

Only because we showed up did we acquire one of the most remarkable photos in *Hiding*: a troupe of Ukrainian entertainers—singers, dancers, musicians—forced to perform for the Nazis, and to pose for the photo. All are staring straight at the camera except my mother, head turned in fear of being recognized. The photo was given to us by the woman who took it. She and her sister had worked with the troupe and read in a Jewish newspaper that we planned to visit the Kharkov Holocaust Museum. We were stunned when they introduced themselves and presented us with the photo.

Only because we traveled to Kharkov could we visit the home of Zhanna's classmate Nicolai Bogancha (and meet his widow), where his Christian family sheltered the fugitive sisters for two weeks at great peril to their own lives, helping them invent aliases and a new story, before the girls began their long journey from persecution and fear to freedom.

In May 1946, when Zhanna and Frina boarded the SS *Marine Flasher*, which carried some eight hundred Holocaust survivors for the voyage to America, all she brought from her life in Ukraine was the sheet music for her beloved *Fantaisie-Impromptu*, five perishable sheets she had miraculously preserved through five years of war. She brought no hope of ever being reunited with family or friends.

One day sixty years later, my mother answered the phone in her Atlanta condo. A woman speaking English with a heavy Russian accent said she was Tamara, her cousin, calling from Israel, where her family had settled after the war. She had been trying to find Zhanna for decades, Tamara said. My mother was skeptical, suspecting an imposter, but Tamara persisted and made her believe. Tamara sent her the family photos subsequently used in *Hiding* and *Alias Anna*. It was the first time I had seen photos of my mother as a child and my grandparents, Dmitri and Sara. When we visited Tamara in Israel, she gave us more photos which expanded the picture of my mother's life—and mine.

Nearly eighty years after Nazis banged on her door in Kharkov, pieces of my mother's fragmented story continued to appear, fruit of our research and publication of the books. In 2018, I had a Facebook message from a stranger in Ukraine, a Ludmila. She explained that her mother, Svetlana, had been a friend of Zhanna's and lived on the same street. Before the Jews were marched away to the tractor factory, Zhanna gave Svetlana her blue silk concert dress for safekeeping.

After escaping the death march to Drobitsky Yar, Zhanna returned to get the dress, but on the way out the door a matching sash "dropped unnoticed and was left with me forever," said Ludmila, recalling her mother's words.

"Forever" ended in 2019. Svetlana's granddaughter, Kate, who lives in Brooklyn with her Russian husband,

Dmitri, visited her mother in Kharkov that summer and returned with the blue silk sash. A short time later the precious cargo arrived by mail at my mother's home in Atlanta. The sash and *Fantaisie* sheet music—the only remnants of the life she lost—have become our most treasured possessions.

Zhanna's beloved sheet music from Chopin's Fantaisie-Impromptu *and the sash to the dress she gave her friend Svetlana for safekeeping. Photo credit: Candy Dawson*

On our next visit to Atlanta we sat with my mother as her still nimble pianist's hands caressed the silk. By then, at age ninety-two, dementia had largely silenced her speech and dimmed her memory, but as she ran her fingers through the silk, she nodded and smiled with a faraway look in her eyes. And I thought of the last thing she told me in our many hours revisiting the past.

"Somehow the story, the history, went around us instead of through us. It is a miraculous thing because anything could have been done to us at any moment in those five years. We did not remain the same, I assure you."

Nor did we.

THE PIECES
ZHANNA AND FRINA PLAYED

ZHANNA'S SOLOS

Beethoven
Appassionata Sonata
Egmont Overture
Pathétique Sonata

Brahms
Hungarian Dances

Chopin
Étude in F Minor, op. 10
Étude No. 5, op. 10
Fantaisie-Impromptu in C-sharp Minor, op. 66
Nocturne No. 1, op. 9
Scherzo in B-flat Minor, op. 31
Waltz Brilliant in A-flat Major, op. 34
Waltz No. 14 in E Minor

Grieg
Piano Concerto in A Minor, op. 16

Liszt
Chasse-Neige, Transcendental Étude No. 12
Hungarian Rhapsody No. 11

Mendelssohn
Scherzo à Capriccio

Rachmaninoff
Prelude in C-sharp Minor

FRINA'S SOLOS

Beethoven
Sonata in D Minor, op. 31 ("The Tempest")

Chopin
Nocturne No. 1, op. 9
Étude in F Minor, op. 10

Grieg
Peer Gynt Suite

Liszt
Hungarian Rhapsody No. 2

Rachmaninoff
Prelude in G Minor

Schubert
Military Marches, op. 51

HITLER, STALIN, AND MUSIC
FASCINATING FACTS

Throughout World War II, music was used as both a weapon and a balm by dictators and citizens alike. Hitler and Stalin greatly increased access to "approved" music and used it as an important propaganda tool to rally and manipulate their people and to assert their racial and cultural superiority. For Resistance fighters, prisoners of war, and people like Zhanna and Frina, music was a way to protest, to communicate, and to survive. A way to stay human in the face of great suffering.

- In 1933, Hitler appointed Joseph Goebbels as the minister of public enlightenment and propaganda. Goebbels greatly increased the number of music halls available to the public and introduced a low-cost radio, "the people's receiver." He used both to spread Nazi-approved music and propaganda. Jewish musicians were thrown out of orchestras and banned from the radio.

- Classical German composers Bach and Beethoven were highly favored, especially music that applauded a patriotic past.

- Chopin was born in Poland, but in 1944, the Germans declared that he was German, of course, because they claimed he was descended from an old Alsatian family named Schopping.

- Jazz and other "degenerate music" was banned by Hitler and Stalin, as were composers of enemy nations such as Claude Debussy, Igor Stravinsky, and Maurice Ravel.

- From 1946 to 1964, music banned by the Soviets was secretly recorded on "bone records," X-ray film discarded by hospitals, thanks to an invention by Ruslan Bogoslowski.

- Hitler's favorite composer was Richard Wagner (1818–1883), who was intensely anti-Semitic.

- Hitler's personal music collection uncovered in a Moscow attic "included Russian composers labeled by the Nazis as 'subhuman' such as Peter Tchaikovsky, Alexander Borodin and Sergei Rachmaninoff."

- The Composers' Union and the Writers' Union in the USSR got to work composing songs for the masses to boost morale and stir up patriotism. To the Soviets, music was a mighty weapon, a way to rally the people and armed forces and to assert the greatness of the Slavic culture that the Nazis defiled and called "subhuman."

- Soviet composer Dmitri Shostakovich took a job as a rooftop firefighter, sweeping incendiary bombs off the top of the Leningrad Conservatory. It was there that he began writing his renowned Symphony No. 7, a testament to the twenty-seven million Soviets who lost their lives in World War II.

- The score for Shostakovich's Symphony No. 7 was smuggled to America and the rest of the world on microfilm. Performed and broadcast to thousands in America, the heartfelt symphony boosted American sympathies for Russian suffering and led to quadrupling American aid to the Soviet war effort in one year. Astonishingly, this music score translated into donations of airplanes, tanks, ammunition, medicine, and food that helped end the war.

- Chopin requested that upon his death, his heart be

buried in his native Poland. His sister smuggled it from Paris to Warsaw, where it was buried under a church monument and became a rallying point for nationalists. During World War II, the Nazis stole it and outlawed his music. It was returned to the church after the war.

FIELD TRIPS AND PLACES OF NOTE

Frederick Collection, Ashburnham, Massachusetts: A small museum where you can view and play an astounding collection of historic pianos dating from 1790 to 1920, including the same model Chopin played.

www.frederickcollection.org

Holocaust Museums, United States: You can visit many Holocaust memorials and museums across the country. Find them listed by state here:

www.en.wikipedia.org/wiki/List_of_Holocaust
_memorials_and_museums_in_the_United_States

Metropolitan Museum of Art, New York, New York: One of three remaining pianofortes made by Bartolomeo Cristofori, the man credited with inventing the piano around 1700.

www.metmuseum.org/toah/hd/cris/hd_cris.htm

Morgan Library, New York, New York: Music manuscripts by Bach, Brahms, Beethoven, Chopin, Liszt, and many others spanning six centuries and many countries are available online.

www.themorgan.org/collection/music-manuscripts
-and-printed-music

Steinway Factory, Astoria, New York: See how Steinway pianos are still handmade on a factory tour. For ages sixteen and up.

www.steinway.com/about/factory-tour

POETRY NOTES

Most of this book is written in *free verse*, which has no set meter or rhyme scheme. However, it uses poetic techniques, such as alliteration, anaphora, assonance, onomatopoeia, refrains, rhythm, and so on. Other poetic forms used in this book are as follows:

"A Candy-Coated Childhood" (p. 10) is a *tercet*, a poem with stanzas of three lines. They can rhyme or not.

"Burdens and Blessings" (p. 13) is a *list poem*, a descriptive list with specific details that define a person, place, thing, or experience.

"Testing" (p. 29) is written in *couplets*, stanzas of two lines each. Couplets can rhyme, but they don't have to.

"Five-Year Plan" (p. 44) is a *cinquain*, a form of poetry composed of five lines with a pattern of two, four, six, eight, and two syllables.

"*S* for Slaughtered by Stalin" (p. 48) is an *ABC poem*, which uses words with initial letters from *A* to *Z*. A similar type of poem is an *acrostic*, in which the first letter of each line spells out the subject of the poem when read from top to bottom.

"What Goes Around Comes Around" (p. 50) is a *reverso poem*, a form invented by Marilyn Singer. The poem reads one way going down and presents another idea or point of view when the same lines are read going up.

"Elegy" (p. 87) is named for its form. An *elegy* is a poetry form used to praise or mourn the dead, so it often has a sad or somber tone. Elegies follow no set pattern.

"True Terror" (p. 92) is a *triolet*, an eight-line poem in which line one repeats as lines four and seven and line two repeats as line eight. The rhyme scheme is ABaAabAB; the capital letters show lines that repeat.

"Awakened" (p. 106) is a *haiku*, a traditional Japanese form of unrhymed poetry, originally written as one vertical line and measured in morae, or breaths. Haiku taught in English usually have three phrases or lines and a set structure: five syllables in the first line, seven in the second, and five in the third. Haiku are keen observations about single moments in time written in present tense; they refer to the natural world and often allude to season or time of day.

"Pyramid Scheme" (p. 116) is a *concrete* or *shape poem*, where words are arranged to form a picture of the subject of the poem. It can rhyme or not.

"Pain" (p. 128) is a *lyric poem*, a broad category that can include a variety of poetic formats, but it's a short, private expression of emotion or powerful feelings. This one uses two quatrains and a couplet.

"What They Left Behind" (p. 143) is a *nonet*, a poem of nine lines. The first line has nine syllables, the second eight, and so on, until the last line ends with one syllable.

"Traveling On" (p. 163) is a *found poem*, which can take existing text found in signs, newspaper articles, graffiti, letters—any text—and use selected words to create a poem. The poet can add or delete text, change the lines or spacing, or leave the words unchanged. It's like a word collage. In this poem, each line is the title of a popular World War II song in the Soviet Union.

"Spinning Secrets" (p. 191) is a rhyming *quatrain*, a form that has one or more four-line stanzas. It's also a shape poem.

"Ode to Victory" (p. 243) is an *ode*, which means it celebrates a person, animal, object, or idea. It often has no formal structure and may or may not rhyme.

SOURCES

I am indebted to my co-author, Zhanna's son Greg Dawson, and his in-depth research tracing his mother's past. Reviewing the mother-son interviews, I was often astonished at how articulate and poetic Zhanna was in her off-the-cuff comments. This book relies on Greg's primary sources, including more than one hundred pages of interviews with his mom, family letters, emails, photographs, videos, a reparations statement, her oral histories as well as his adult books *Hiding in the Spotlight* and *Judgment Before Nuremberg*.

I first met Greg in Florida, where he and his wife Candy shared Zhanna's astounding story, memorabilia, and a video of their trip to Ukraine and Israel that shows his mother's house, piano school, and friends who helped Zhanna and her sister escape. It was fascinating. When I got up to go, none of us realized that we had been talking for five hours! We continued talking all that spring and decided we wanted to work in concert to tell Zhanna's story to a younger audience, to kids Zhanna's and Frina's age when they first escaped. I suggested a biography in verse to echo the music that played such a big part of their lives.

Other sources include secondary sources: books, websites, museum files, and films. Zhanna has been interviewed by Steven Spielberg's Shoah Project, for the Yad Vashem World Holocaust Remembrance Center in Israel, and for the National WWII Museum in the U.S. (See websites, a bibliography, and more on pages 328-335.)

QUOTE SOURCES

Zhanna's quotes throughout the book came from interviews with her son Greg Dawson and from Zhanna's oral history recorded by the William Breman Jewish Heritage Museum. All other quote sources are as follows:

Page vii: *"Music gave us so much . . ."* Nurit Jugend, "Music During the Holocaust." *They Played for Their Lives.* www.theyplayedfortheirlives.com

Page vii: *"Can music attack evil?"* Solomon Volkov, *Testimony: The Memoirs of Dmitri Shostakovich.* Pompton Plains, NJ: Limelight Editions, 2004: 234.

Page 67: *"Life is getting merrier . . ."* Joseph Stalin, at the First All-Union Meeting of Stakhanovites on November 17, 1935.

Page 73: *"Zhanna was slim as a young birch tree . . ."* Irina Vlodavskaya interview with Greg Dawson.

Page 75: *"Citizens of the Soviet Union!"* Vyacheslav Molotov.

"Molotov: Reaction to German Invasion of 1941."

sourcebooks.fordham.edu/mod/1941molotov.asp

Page 81: *"fight to the last drop of blood"*; *"must not be left a single engine, a single railway truck . . ."*; *"blow up bridges and roads . . ."* Joseph Stalin (n.d.). Radio broadcast, from

www.marxists.org/reference/archive/stalin/works/1941/07/03.htm

Page 93: *"All the night the reaper reaps . . ."* Taras Shevchenko. "The Reaper."

www.infoukes.com/shevchenkomuseum/poetry.htm

Page 120: *"Please let my little girl go."* Dmitri Arshansky, Zhanna interview with Greg Dawson.

Page 122: *"I don't care what you do. Just live."* Dmitri Arshansky, Zhanna interview with Greg Dawson.

Page 157: *"Sie sind Kinder!"* Zhanna Arshankaya interview with Greg Dawson.

Page 203: *"Not a step back!"* History.com Editors. "Battle of Stalingrad," November 9, 2009.

www.history.com/topics/world-war-ii/battle-of-stalingrad

Page 245: Newspaper headlines: "Nazis Quit" (*New York Post*, May 7, 1945), "Surrender Is Unconditional" (*New York Times*, May 8, 1945), "V-E Day—It's All Over" (*Daily Mail*, May 8, 1945).

Page 266: *"If you could have anything you desired . . ."* Larry Dawson, Zhanna interview with Greg Dawson.

Page 267: *"You're part of my family now."* Larry Dawson, Zhanna interview with Greg Dawson.

Page 286: *"In Ukraine there are no Jews."* Journalist Vassily Grossman. Quoted in Lorraine Boissoneault, "The WWII Massacres at Drobitsky Yar Were the Result of Years of Scapegoating Jews," December 15, 2016. www.smithsonianmag.com/history/wwii-massacres-drobitsky -yar-were-result-years-scapegoating-jews-180961466/

Page 287: *"The wild grasses rustle over Babi Yar..."* Yevgeny Yevtushenko. Excerpted with the permission of Marie Yevtushenko.

WEBSITES

Author Greg Dawson:

www.gregdawsonbooks.com

Official *Hiding in the Spotlight* book website:

Hiding in the Spotlight: A True Holocaust Story.

www.hidinginthespotlight.com

Oral History—Zhanna tells her story in her own words:

"Arshanskaya, Zhanna." The William Breman Jewish Heritage Museum.

www.thebreman.org/Research/Cuba-Family-Archives /Oral-Histories/ID/816/Arshanskaya-Zhanna

More about Frina, her husband, and their music careers:

"Arschanska and Boldt."

www.arschanskaandboldt.com

Steven Spielberg's Shoah Project: A video of Zhanna's 1995 testimony is on the project website, but viewable only at certain museums/libraries such as Yale University.

www.sfi.usc.edu/

United States Holocaust Memorial Museum:

www.ushmm.org.

World War II Museum: A 2 1/2-hour interview with Zhanna.

www.ww2online.org/view/zhanna-dawson#final-thoughts

ABOUT THE "HOLOCAUST BY BULLETS"

Bazyler, Michael J., and Kellyanne Rose Gold. "The Judicialization of International Atrocity Crimes: The Kharkov Trial of 1943."

www.core.ac.uk/download/pdf/160257601.pdf

DesBois, P. (n.d.). "The Shooting of Jews in Ukraine: Holocaust by Bullets."

www.mjhnyc.org/exhibitions/shooting-jews-ukraine-holocaust -bullets/ and https://encyclopedia.ushmm.org/content/en /article/documenting-numbers-of-victims-of-the-holocaust

-and-nazi-persecution and https://encyclopedia.ushmm.org
/content/en/article/kiev-and-babi-yar

"Documenting Numbers of Victims of the Holocaust and Nazi Persecution." (n.d.).
www.encyclopedia.ushmm.org/content/en/article
/documenting-numbers-of-victims-of-the-holocaust-and-nazi
-persecution

Drobitsky Yar.
www.drobytskyyar.org/index.php?form_page=1&lang=en

"Kiev and Babi Yar." (n.d.)
www.encyclopedia.ushmm.org/content/en/article/kiev-and
-babi-yar

SOURCES FOR HITLER, STALIN, AND MUSIC: FASCINATING FACTS

Nazis Claim Chopin was a German:
www.timesmachine.nytimes.com/timesmachine/1944
/05/05/96411002.html?pageNumber=5

Bone records:
www.npr.org/2016/01/09/462289635/bones-and-grooves

-weird-secret-history-of-soviet-x-ray-music

Hitler's secret music collection:

www.dw.com/en/hitlers-unearthed-music-collection-yields
-surprising-finds/a-2722872

Chopin's heart:

https://www.atlasobscura.com/articles/chopins-heart
-exhumed-for-a-top-secret-check-up.

NEWS REPORTS

NEWS REPORTS

Basu, Moni. "Playing to Live: Pianist Survived Holocaust by Performing for Nazis." CNN, May 12, 2012.
www.edition.cnn.com/2012/05/12/us/georgia-holocaust-survivor/index.html

Dawson, Greg. "Hiding in Spotlight, Jewish Pianist Survived WWII." NPR, September 12, 2009.
www.npr.org/templates/story/story.php?storyId=112728395

Dawson, Greg. "A Return to Ukraine." OrlandoSentinel.com, July 16, 2009.
www.orlandosentinel.com/entertainment/orl-greg-dawson-travels-to-ukraine-071909-story.html

FILMS

Film and Q&A with Zhanna, Greg, Candy, and Aimée Dawson

"Greg Dawson: From Ukraine to Juilliard; a Piano Prodigy's Holocaust Odyssey." Rollins College. www.rollins.edu/rollins-winter-park-institute/events /2010-2011/greg-dawson.html

Movie: The true story of the Welsh journalist who broke the news about the Holodomor

Mr. Jones. Directed by Agnieszka Holland, performances by James Norton, Vanessa Kirby, Peter Sarsgaard. Film Produkcja, Crab Apple Films. 2019. Available on Amazon Prime.

BIBLIOGRAPHY

Anderson, M. T. *Symphony for the City of the Dead: Dmitri Shostakovich and the Siege of Leningrad.* Somerville, MA: Candlewick Press, 2015.

Dawson, Greg. *Hiding in the Spotlight: A Musical Prodigy's Story of Survival, 1941–1946.* New York: Pegasus Books, 2009.

Dawson, Greg. *Judgment Before Nuremberg: The Holocaust in the Ukraine and the First Nazi War Crimes Trial.* New York: Pegasus Books, 2012.

LaFarge, Annik. *Chasing Chopin: A Musical Journey Across Three Centuries, Four Countries, and a Half-Dozen Revolutions.* New York: Simon & Schuster, 2020.

Snyder, Timothy. *Bloodlands: Europe Between Hitler and Stalin.* New York: Basic Books, 2010.

WITH GRATITUDE

Endless, heartfelt thanks to the Dawson family for sharing this astounding true story. Greg's, Candy's, and Aimée's generous, thoughtful, and funny responses to all my questions made writing this book an extraordinary collaboration and Zhanna's no-nonsense courage inspired me throughout the scary months of the COVID-19 pandemic. I'm grateful to Dr. Jürgen Matthäus of the United States Holocaust Memorial Museum; to Rabbi James Prosnit; to photographers Patrick Breslin and Tanya Zaharchenko; to Maria, Sasha, and Zhenya Yevtushenko; and to illustrators Anna and Elena Balbusso for sharing their talent and expertise. Thanks to Misty Beyer; Eve Catarevas; Karlin Gray and her son Gabriel; Caroline, Jack, and Grace Gueterman; Barbara and Jim Harman; Karen Jordan; Susan Montanari; and Joan Riordan for weighing in on the manuscript, music notes, or cover options. As always, I'm indebted to my brilliant agent, Brenda Bowen, and the dream team at HarperCollins—Nancy Inteli, Megan Ilnitzki, Erika DiPasquale, Laura Mock, Joel Tippie, Laura Harshberger, Mark Rifkin, Emma Meyer, Mimi Rankin, Patty Rosati, and Aubrey Churchward! And finally, here's to my husband, Paul, and my daughters, Emily and Allison, for listening, reading, fact-checking, helping me solve historical puzzles, rereading, and on and on. I can't thank them enough for their endless love and support.

—Susan Hood

Alias Anna is not just another iteration of my mother's story. It's an extension of her legacy, a legacy she never sought but created as teller of a story shedding light on a lost chapter of the Holocaust, the dawn hours in Ukraine. Susan Hood's ingenious retelling of *Hiding in the Spotlight* —which I wrote for adult readers—is the answer to my mother's question, "How can you tell children about such things?" This is how: with rhythmic, accessible verse in service of a faithful abridging of the story for youthful sensibilities.

Alias Anna brings the story of the Shoah in Ukraine to a vast new audience, arguably the most important one of all, the next generation to inherit the world and become keepers of the flame. "Never again." This important contribution to Holocaust literature is due to three remarkable women:

my daughter, Aimée, for writing the letter that persuaded her grandmother to break her long silence; my mother's courage in recounting an unspeakable ordeal; and my wife, Candy, for getting me to the word processor, believing in my ability to tell the story when I didn't.

—Greg Dawson